CHINESE
Characters
in Pictures

(1)

汪　春　郑重庆 编著

曹伟业　　插图绘画

华语教学出版社

SINOLINGUA

First Edition 2005
Fourth Printing 2012

ISBN 978-7-80200-101-5
Copyright 2005 by Sinolingua Co., Ltd
Published by Sinolingua Co., Ltd
24 Baiwanzhuang Road, Beijing 100037, China
Tel: (86) 10-68320585 68997826
Fax: (86) 10-68997826 68326333
http://www.sinolingua.com.cn
E-mail: hyjx@sinolingua.com.cn
Facebook: www.facebook.com/sinolingua
Printed by Beijing Mixing Printing Co., Ltd

Printed in the People's Republic of China

Preface

The American poet Ezra Pound once said, "The easiest language in the world for writing poetry is Chinese." And in the words of E. E. Cummings, another American poet, "Chinese poets are painters." This book, *Chinese Characters in Pictures* is one which uses words to explain and pictures to illustrate the form and structure of Chinese characters. Therefore, it is both a collection of poetry and a picture album, so to speak.

Each Chinese character has a form of its own, representing a particular sound and a particular meaning, one at least. In other words, each character is a unity of form, sound and meaning. The student of Chinese must call on every one of the individuals if he or she is to really know the personality of each.

Learning Chinese is quite different from learning any other language. The way of learning is different. In learning a Western language, for instance, you swallow a whole series of sounds, lock, stock and barrel. If you were to take a word apart, separating it into so many phonetic syllables, it would lose its meaning altogether. In learning Chinese, however, what you have to do is exactly that, not into so many syllables, but into so many characters. You learn first the characters, then the word. Take, for instance, the Chinese word 大学 (dà xué) which means "university". You first learn the words 大 and 学 separately since 大学 is formed by combining the two characters (you might call them elements of language). In meaning, 大学 has to do with both 大 and 学, and yet 大学 is not a simple case of 大 plus 学. 大学 is the Chinese equivalent of the English word "university". But if you were to take the English word "university" and try to figure out its meaning based on the meanings of the five syllabic components u/ni/ver/si/ty, you would definitely get nowhere, because separately, these components have no meaning at all and certainly have nothing to do with what the word "university" means. So, the character forms the basis in learning Chinese, whereas the word or sentence forms the basis for learning a Western language. It is no wonder then that there should have been so many textbooks written since ancient times on learning Chinese characters, e.g. *Qian Zi Wen* (Learn A Thousand Characters) and *Bai Jia Xing* (One Hundred Family Names).

The pictures as represented in the Chinese characters vary in complexity. Take the characters contained in this book. Some are as simple as 人,口,牛,羊; others as complicated as 双, 养, 喜, 声. Whether simple or complicated, they are each a picture and a poem. Of course, one cannot expect everyone to agree in their analyses of each and every character, just as people couldn't totally agree, in fact they might totally disagree, in their understanding and interpretation of a painting or a poem. Regardless of whether the poet or painter agrees or disagrees, the reader or viewer would have his own appreciation of the work on the basis of his or her own understanding. The same holds true, more or less, for the written script. It is your right to create the written character, it is my right to interpret it.

Chinese Characters in Pictures is written for those non-Chinese who intend to explore the secrets of the civilization. It is somewhat like a guidebook, listing nearly two hundred cultural sites. Like the looking glass in *Alice in Wonderland,* the characters depicted in this book will take the tourist into the kaleidoscopic world that is Chinese culture.

by Cheng Xianghui
Dean of College of Chinese Language
University of Macao

前言

美国诗人埃兹拉·庞德曾经说过:"世界上最适合写诗的语言是汉语。"美国另一位诗人E.E.卡明斯说:"中国诗人都是画家。"《画说汉字》用语言诠释、用图画演示汉字的结构和字形,因此可以说:这本书既是诗集又是画册。

每个汉字都有其独特的字形、特别的发音和至少一个字义。换句话说,每个汉字都是字形、声音和意义的统一体。学习汉语的学生必须接触每一个汉字才能真正了解它们的个性。

学习汉语的方法不同于学习其他语言。例如在西方语言中,若干个毫无意义的音节构成一个词,如果你把一个词拆分成音节,它的意义就不复存在。但是学习汉语则不同,你要做的恰恰是把一个词拆分成独立的字,在学习词之前先要学习字。以汉语"大学"(university)为例,你先要分别学习"大"和"学"这两个字,因为"大学"这个词是由这两个字组成的(你可以称它们为"语素")。从词义上看,"大学"和"大"和"学"有关系,但并不等于"大"和"学"这两个字义的简单相加。和"大学"对应的英文是university,如果你试图通过这个英文单词的五个音节u/ni/ver/si/ty推断出它的意思,那将是白费力气,因为这些音节没有意义,和词义毫无关联。词或句子是西方语言的基本元素,而汉语的基本元素是汉字。正是因为如此,从古至今,学习汉字的书层出不穷,如:《千字文》,《百家姓》等。

用以表示汉字的图形繁简不一。拿这本书中涉及的字来说,有些非常简单,象"人"、"口"、"牛"、"羊",有些却非常复杂,象"双"、"养"、"喜"、"声"。不论简单还是复杂,每一个字都象是一幅画、一首诗。也许并非所有人都赞同本书中对每个汉字的诠释,就象每个人对诗歌或绘画都有不同的理解一样,不论原创者有着怎样的寓意,读者或观者总是会在欣赏时加入自己的理解,对汉字的理解也或多或少地符合这一规则。

《**画**说汉字》是为那些希望探究中国文明史的外国朋友编写的,它就象一本旅游手册,带领读者徜徉于近200个"文化名胜";书中的汉字就象《爱丽斯漫游奇境》中的魔镜,引导旅游者进入中国文化的万花筒。

程祥徽
澳门大学汉语学院院长

Contents

ān

(peaceful; quiet; calm)

`	`	宀	宀	安	安

　　"安"（）字的外面（宀）是一间屋子，屋里有一个弯着腰的女子（）。以前，人们认为女人留在家中料理一切事务，就会有安定的生活。

This character is comprised of two parts: the outer portion is a house (宀). Inside the house there is a bowing woman (女) facing towards the left. "A woman stays inside the house" has long been considered the condition of peace, the earliest known meaning of this particular pictograph.

【部首】 Radical　　宀(roof)

【同部首字】 Characters under the radical
　　宋(a surname)， 宜(suitable)， 宝(treasure)

【词语】 Words and phrases

安定	āndìng	stable; settled
安分	ānfèn	be law-abiding
安好	ānhǎo	safe and sound; well
安静	ānjìng	quiet; peaceful
安全	ānquán	safe; secure
安慰	ānwèi	to comfort

安分守己
　　　ān fèn shǒu jǐ
　　　　keep one's duty and be self-restrained
　　　　　　i.e., act properly according to one's status

安居乐业
　　　ān jū lè yè
　　　　live and work in peace and contentment

安然无恙
ān rán wú yàng
　　　　safe and sound
　　　　　　i.e., (escape)unscathed

安如泰山
　　　ān rú tài shān
　　　　as secure as Mount Taishan

安不忘危
　　　ān bú wàng wēi
　　　　mindful of possible danger in time of peace

【例句】Example
　　　祝你一路平安!
　　　　zhù nǐ yí lù píng ān
　　　　　　Have a good trip!

八

bā

(eight)

　　"八"字笔划较少，以前用它表示把东西分为两份，所以有"分开"或"分别"的意思。后来"分开"这个意思被用作数字的"八"取代了，这个数字便一直沿用至今。"八"也可做部首，以"八"为部首的字多数包含"分开"的意思。

　　The character 八 seems very simple. Yet, it is a combined representation which shows one thing being divided or parted into two halves. So originally 八 meant "divide" or "part". But later the meaning of "divide" was completely lost. 八 came to mean the number "eight", which has nothing to do with the original meaning. 八 is also a radical. Most Chinese characters formed with 八 have something to do with the meaning of "divide".

【部首】Radical　　八(eight)

【同部首字】Characters under the radical
　　兵(soldier)，典(standard)

【词语】Words and phrases

八成	bāchéng	eighty percent
八度	bādù	octave
八方	bāfāng	the eight points of the compass; all directions
八卦	bāguà	the "Eight Diagrams" (eight combinations of three whole or broken lines formerly used in divination)

八仙	bāxiān	the "Eight Immortals" (in the legend)
八月	bāyuè	August

八方呼应

bā fāng hū yìng

respond from all sides

八方支援

bā fāng zhī yuán

help from all quarters

八面玲珑

bā miàn líng lóng

manage to please everybody

八十岁学吹打

bā shí suì xué chuī dǎ

learn to pipe and drum at the age of eighty

i.e., never too old to learn

八仙过海，各显神通

bā xiān guò hǎi, gè xiǎn shén tōng

like the Eight Immortals crossing the sea, each one showing his or her special prowess

【例句】Example

我买了八本中文书。

wǒ mǎi le bā běn zhōng wén shū

I bought eight Chinese books.

bái

(white)

在象形字里，（白）看上去有一个光环正围绕着一团熊熊烈火，给人光亮的感觉，后来它还带有"清澈"、"清晰"、"清楚"的意义。

The original meaning of 白 is brightness. In the oracle bones, it is a picture of a fire burning with a bright ring surrounding it. Later it evolved to mean "clarity" or "clearness".

【部首】Radical　　　白(white)

【同部首字】Characters under the radical
皇(imperial)，的(a particle)，皎(clear and bright)

【词语】Words and phrases

白菜	báicài	Chinese cabbage
白痴	báichī	idiocy
白饭	báifàn	plain cooked rice
白费	báifèi	waste
白宫	báigōng	the White House
白色	báisè	white (colour)
白天	báitiān	daytime; day
白银	báiyín	silver

白璧无瑕

    bái bì wú xiá

       flawless white jade

          i.e., impeccable moral integrity

白费心思

    bái fèi xīn sī

       to rack one's brains in vain

白驹过隙

    bái jū guò xì

       like glimpsing white colt flashing past a chink in the wall

          i.e., time flies

白日做梦

    bái rì zuò mèng

       daydream

白头偕老

    bái tóu xié lǎo

       remain a devoted couple to the end of their lives

白日不做亏心事，夜半敲门心不惊

    bái rì bú zuò kuī xīn shì, yè bàn qiāo mén xīn bù jīng

       A clear conscience laughs at false accusations.

【例句】 Example

    她听到这个消息顿时脸色苍白。

       tā tīng dào zhè gè xiāo xī dùn shí liǎn sè cāng bái

          She went as white as sheet when she heard the news.

běn

(the root of a plant; foundation)

一	十	才	木	本

　　汉字的确很神奇，在"木"（朩）字底部加上一画后，就变成了"本"字。"本"是指树木的根部，后来慢慢发展为"所有事物的根本"，同时也有"自己"的意思。

An additional short stroke is put near the base of the character 木(朩), originally meaning"tree", it is to emphasize where the roots of the tree are. So,"root" is the original meaning of 本. It extends to mean the foundation for all the things. From the meaning of "foundation" , it also extends to mean "one's own".

【部首】Radical　　　木(tree)

【同部首字】Characters under the radical
　　　材(material)，村(village)，杜(a surname)

【词语】Words and phrases

本国	běnguó	one's own country
本能	běnnéng	instinct
本钱	běnqián	capital
本人	běnrén	me; myself; oneself
本土	běntǔ	one's native country
本性	běnxìng	natural instincts
本意	běnyì	original meaning

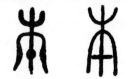

本源　　　　　běnyuán　　　　origin; source

本固枝荣

　　běn gù zhī róng

　　　　When the root is firm, the branches flourish.

本末倒置

　　běn mò dào zhì

　　　　take the branch for the root

　　　　　　i.e., put the cart before the horse

本地姜不辣

　　běn dì jiāng bú là

　　　　Local ginger is not peppery.

　　　　　　i.e., Familiarity diminishes appreciation.

本来面目

　　běn lái miàn mù

　　　　true colour

　　　　　　i.e., true features

本乡本土

　　běn xiāng běn tǔ

　　　　one's native land

　　　　　　i.e., one's hometown

【例句】Example

　　助人是快乐之本。

　　　　zhù rén shì kuài lè zhī běn

　　　　　　Helping people is the foundation of happiness.

比

bǐ

(compare; close to)

一　上　比　比

　　你能看出这个字（𣏾）里有两个人站得很近吗？它所指的意义很多，原先是"亲近"、"亲密"的意思，后来两个人站着比高低，就有"比较"、"对照"等意思了。你听过一句世代相传的诗文："海内存知己，天涯若比邻"吗？它是说人们无论走到哪里都要记着友情的可贵，到了天涯海角，彼此的心都靠得很近。

　　This character originally shows two people standing together facing towards the right (𣏾), very close to each other, giving us the original meaning of "close", as we can see from the well-known verse：海内存知己，天涯若比邻 (Keeping good friends in mind wherever they roam, even to the ends of the earth, you would feel them as close as next door.). Over time it has evolved and acquired the additional meanings of "compare" as in 比较 and 对比, as well as 比喻.

【部首】Radical　　　比(compare)

【同部首字】Characters under the radical
　　　毗(adjoin)，毕(finish)，皆(all)

【词语】Words and phrases
比较	bǐjiào	comparison; contrast; relatively
比邻	bǐlín	next-door neighbour
比率	bǐlǜ	rate;ratio

比如	bǐrú	for example; for instance; such as
比赛	bǐsài	competition; match
比喻	bǐyù	metaphor

比比皆是

    bǐ bǐ jiē shì

        can be found everywhere

比肩而事

    bǐ jiān ér shì

        work shoulder to shoulder

比翼双飞

    bǐ yì shuāng fēi

        fly side by side

比上不足，比下有余

    bǐ shàng bù zú, bǐ xià yǒu yú

        One man may fall short of the best but be better than the worst.

无可比拟

    wú kě bǐ nǐ

        beyond compare

            i.e., incomparable; matchless

【例句】Example

    来，我俩比一比!

        lái, wǒ liǎ bǐ yì bǐ

            Come on, let's have a competition!

笔

bǐ

(pen)

| 丿 | 𠂉 | 𠂉 | 𠂉 | 竹 | 竹 | 竿 | 笔 | 笔 | 笔 |

古时的"笔"()是由手()和笔杆()组成，你看它像不像一只拿着笔的手呢？古时的"笔"是用"竹"和"毛"制成的，这就是"毛笔"了。

This was originally an ideogram. In the oracle bones, the upper right part of the character is a hand ( ), and the left side in the shape of a pen ( ) represents the body of the pen. The character underwent numerous changes. In regular script it has lost most of its resemblance to a pen, but interestingly, in simplified Chinese, is written as 笔, a combination of 竹 " bamboo" and 毛 " hair" which is exactly what a Chinese pen was made of.

【部首】Radical　　竹(bamboo)

【同部首字】Characters under the radical
笨(stupid)，算(calculate)，筋(tendon)

【词语】Words and phrases

笔法	bǐfǎ	technique of writing
笔迹	bǐjì	a person's handwriting
笔录	bǐlù	take down (in writing); record
笔名	bǐmíng	pen name
笔墨	bǐmò	pen and ink; words
笔试	bǐshì	written examination

笔译　　　　bǐyì　　　　written translation

妙笔生花
　　miào bǐ shēng huā
　　　　Flowers spring up under one's pen.
　　　　　　i.e., have great literary talent

笔飞墨舞
　　bǐ fēi mò wǔ
　　　　The pen flies, the ink dances.
　　　　　　i.e., write quickly

笔耕度日
　　bǐ gēng dù rì
　　　　making a living by writing

笔剑唇枪
　　bǐ jiàn chún qiāng
　　　　The pen is as sharp as the sword and the tongue as the spear.

笔墨官司
　　bǐ mò guān si
　　　　written polemics

笔墨难罄
　　bǐ mò nán qìng
　　　　hard to describe by pen and ink
　　　　　　i.e., beyond description

【例句】Example
　　这枝笔是一位中国朋友送我的礼物。
　　　　zhè zhī bǐ shì yí wèi zhōng guó péng yǒu sòng wǒ de lǐ wù
　　　　　　This pen is a gift from a Chinese friend.

bīng

(ice)

丶　冫　冫丨　冫刂　冰　冰

冰（）是由水凝结而成的。"水"是后来加上去的（冰），这就成了现在所写的"冰"了。冰来自于水，人类早就知道！

In the oracle bones this character is in the form of (), like protruding ice pieces, so originally 冰 was a pictographic character. But later a 水 "water" radical was added to it (冰), showing that "ice" is made of "water".

【部首】Radical　　冫(water)

【同部首字】Characters under the radical
决(decide)，冷(cold)，次(time)

【词语】Words and phrases
冰雹	bīngbáo	hail
冰川	bīngchuān	glacier
冰袋	bīngdài	ice bag
冰岛	Bīngdǎo	Iceland
冰冷	bīnglěng	ice-cold
冰山	bīngshān	iceberg

冰天雪地

    bīng tiān xuě dì

        a world of ice and snow

冰消瓦解

    bīng xiāo wǎ jiě

        to melt like ice and break like tiles

冰冻三尺，非一日之寒

    bīng dòng sān chǐ, fēi yí rì zhī hán

        It takes more than one cold day for the river to freeze three feet deep.

            i.e., The trouble has been brewing for quite some time.

【例句】Example

    这水冰手。

        zhè shuǐ bīng shǒu

          This water is freezing cold.

bù

(step; pace; walk)

'	⻌	⺊	止	牛	芾	步

"步" 的原意是 "向前走"。在甲骨文中，步是由两只脚构成的（🐾）。上半部分是左脚，下半部分是右脚，表示两只脚轮流向前移动。"步" 还可以作名词，是古代的长度单位。现在的 "步" 字上半部基本没有太大改变，下半部则完全不同了。

步 is comprised of two feet. In the oracle bones, the upper part is a left foot with the big toe pointing upwards (🐾) and the lower part is a right foot with the big toe also pointing upwards (🐾), but in the other direction. Two feet moving forwards one after another signifies "walking forward", which is the original meaning of 步 "step". It is also used as a noun, and as an old unit of measurement. The modern version of 步 still keeps "the foot" in the upper part, but the lower part of it has been changed completely into another form.

【部首】Radical　　止(stop)

【同部首字】Characters under the radical
肯(willing)，此(this)，耻(shame)

【词语】Words and phrases

步兵	bùbīng	infantry
步步	bùbù	step by step
步调	bùdiào	pace
步枪	bùqiāng	rifle

步行	bùxíng	to walk; go on foot
步骤	bùzhòu	step; move
步子	bùzi	step; pace
散步	sànbù	take a walk

步步高升

bù bù gāo shēng

be promoted step by step

步调一致

bù diào yí zhì

march in step

i.e., act in unison

步人后尘

bù rén hòu chén

follow in somebody's footsteps

步武先贤

bù wǔ xiān xián

tread in the footsteps of the worthies of the past

步步为营

bù bù wéi yíng

advance gradually and entrench oneself at every step

【例句】 Example

只有几步就到家了!

zhǐ yǒu jǐ bù jiù dào jiā le

We're only a few steps away from home now!

草

cǎo

(grass)

| 一 | 十 | 艹 | 艹 | 节 | 芦 | 苩 | 草 | 草 |

"草"的古字上面像两株草（ᵜ），它同时也用作部首。后来人们又在下面加上"早"字以表示它的读音。

The upper part of 草 is a pictograph for grass（ᵜ resembling two blades of grass）which is the origin of this character, and is also a radical for grass or plants. The lower part 早 was later added as a sound component.

【部首】Radical   ⁺⁺(grass)

【同部首字】Characters under the radical
药(medicine)，芳(fragrant)，芽(bud)

【词语】Words and phrases

草地	cǎodì	grassland
草稿	cǎogǎo	draft
草绿	cǎolǜ	grass green
草帽	cǎomào	straw hat
草莓	cǎoméi	strawberry
草棚	cǎopéng	thatched shack
草皮	cǎopí	sod
草坪	cǎopíng	lawn

草率	cǎoshuài	careless
草图	cǎotú	sketch
草药	cǎoyào	medicinal herbs
草约	cǎoyuē	draft treaty
草原	cǎoyuán	prairie

草草过目

cǎo cǎo guò mù

glance over

草草了事

cǎo cǎo liǎo shì

get a job done any old way

草草收场

cǎo cǎo shōu chǎng

hastily wind up a matter

草菅人命

cǎo jiān rén mìng

treat human life as if it were not worth a straw

草莽英雄

cǎo mǎng yīng xióng

a hero of the greenwood

草木皆兵

cǎo mù jiē bīng

see every bush and tree as an enemy

草动知风向

cǎo dòng zhī fēng xiàng

A straw shows which way the wind blows.

【例句】 Example

他在园子里锄草呢。

tā zài yuán zǐ lǐ chú cǎo ne

He is hoeing up weeds in the garden.

chū

(go out; come out)

ノ	ㄩ	屮	出	出

这个字由两部分构成：下半部是一条弧形，代表门口（∨）；上半部是脚和脚趾头的形状（屮），意思是说这只脚要踏出家门工作去了，后又引申为"超过，生产"的意思。记住，这个字不是两座重叠的山！

The original character 出 is a combination of two parts: the lower part is a line which curves upwards indicating a doorway or a cave-dwelling (∨);the upper part is a foot with the toe pointing upwards (屮), implying the foot moving across threshold of the door or cave-dwelling. The original meaning of the character was "to go out" or "to come out"; later it extended to mean "exceed", "produce", etc.

【部首】Radical   凵(frame)

【同部首字】Characters under the radical
　　函(letter)，击(beat)

【词语】Words and phrases
出版	chūbǎn	come off the press; come out; publish
出兵	chūbīng	dispatch troops
出差	chūchāi	be on business
出产	chūchǎn	produce
出丑	chūchǒu	make a fool of oneself

出发	chūfā	set out
出境	chūjìng	leave the country
出口	chūkǒu	speak out; export; exit; utter

出尔反尔

chū ěr fǎn ěr

go back on one's word

出乎意料

chū hū yì liào

contrary to one's expectations

出口成章

chū kǒu chéng zhāng

Words flow from the mouth as from the pen of a master.

i.e., speech full of elegance

出类拔萃

chū lèi bá cuì

stand out from among one's fellows

出生入死

chū shēng rù sǐ

go through fire and water

i.e., risk one's life

出奇制胜

chū qí zhì shèng

achieve the victory through unusual means

出污泥而不染

chū wū ní ér bù rǎn

come out of the mud unsoiled

i.e., emerge unstained from the filth

出其不意，攻其无备

chū qí bú yì, gōng qí wú bèi

do what one does not expect and strike when one is unprepared

【例句】Example

今天早上他出城了。

jīn tiān zǎo shàng tā chū chéng le

He went out of the town this morning.

chū

(beginning)

裁衣服的第一个步骤就是要有"衣"和"刀",这就是"初"字想表达的意思,即"所有事情的开始",例如:最初、起初。

This is an ideogram formed by two pictograms: on the left side is 衣 "clothes" and on the right side is 刀 "knife". Combined, these elements suggest using a knife to tailor new clothes, which in turn stands for the "beginning" of the process of making clothes. Gradually, it was generalized to mean "the beginning" of all things.

【部首】Radical   衤(clothes)

【同部首字】Characters under the radical
补(mend),袖(sleeve),衫(shirt)

【词语】Words and phrases

初步	chūbù	initial
初次	chūcì	the first time
初等	chūděng	elementary
初婚	chūhūn	first marriage
初交	chūjiāo	new acquaintance
初恋	chūliàn	first love
初期	chūqī	initial stage

初出茅庐

    chū chū máo lú

        just come out of one's thatched cottage

            i.e., at the beginning of one's career; young and inexperienced

初露锋芒

    chū lù fēng máng

        display one's talent for the first time

初生牛犊不怕虎

    chū shēng niú dú bú pà hǔ

        New born calves are not afraid of tigers.

            i.e., Young people are fearless.

初入世途

    chū rù shì tú

        start in life

初衷不改

    chū zhōng bù gǎi

        do not change one's original intention

【例句】Example

    初学汉语，要有耐心。

        chū xué hàn yǔ, yào yǒu nài xīn

            It requires much patience in learning Chinese at the beginning.

cóng

(from)

丿 人 从 从

古字的"从"，可以看到一个人正跟着另一个人，两人紧紧地靠在一起（），不难想到有"跟从"的含义。后来渐渐发展成"服从"、"附从"、"从哪里来"等意思。

From early oracle bones, we can see two people standing close together, facing towards the left (彳), one person following the other. So "follow" is the original meaning of this character. Then, by extension and evolution the meaning shifts towards "obedient" and "from", also "accessory".

【部首】Radical　　人(person)

【同部首字】Characters under the radical
今(today)，令(order)，仓(storehouse)

【词语】Words and phrases

从此	cóngcǐ	from now on
从前	cóngqián	before
从事	cóngshì	to be engaged in
从属	cóngshǔ	to be subordinate to
从头	cóngtóu	from the beginning

从古到今

    cóng gǔ dào jīn

      from ancient times to the present

从一而终

    cóng yī ér zhōng

      to be faithful to one's husband to the very end

从善如流

    cóng shàn rú liú

      to follow good advice as naturally as the river follows its course

从长计议

    cóng cháng jì yì

      need further consideration

【例句】 Example

    您从哪儿来?

      nín cóng nǎr lái

        Where are you from?

典

diǎn

(law)

| 丶 | 冂 | 曰 | 曲 | 曲 | 曲 | 典 | 典 |

　　"典"字（燚）就像一双手（乂乀）拿着一本书（卌）在看一样。后来一双手变成了一个书架，书架上放着的当然是书籍。以前"典"是指一些著名书籍，也就是"经典"，而一些著名的医书又叫作"药典"，后又引申出"法规"、"规章"的意思。

　　This character is comprised of (卌) on the top half and two "hands" (乂乀) on the bottom half, signifying books being held in a pair of hands. Later the form of the character was changed by replacing the hands with a (丌)— something like what we call a bookshelf nowadays. So the original meaning for "diǎn" was "important/model books", as nowadays we still say 经典(jīng diǎn: classics) or 药典(yào diǎn: medical classics). From the meaning "classics", it has also been extended to mean "law" or "system".

【部首】Radical　　　　八(eight)

【同部首字】Characters under the radical
　　其(he; that)，具(tool)，共(together)

【词语】Words and phrases

典范	diǎnfàn	model; example
典故	diǎngù	allusion
典籍	diǎnjí	ancient codes and records
典礼	diǎnlǐ	ceremony

| 典型 | diǎnxíng | typical |
| 典雅 | diǎnyǎ | refined; elegant |

典型示范

　　diǎn xíng shì fàn

　　　　show typical examples from real life

典雅可传

　　diǎn yǎ kě chuán

　　　　be refined and worthy of being perpetuated

典章制度

　　diǎn zhāng zhì dù

　　　　(old) laws and institutions

典型人物

　　diǎn xíng rén wù

　　　　a typical character

【例句】Example

　　我买了一本汉英词典。

　　　　wǒ mǎi le yì běn hàn yīng cí diǎn

　　　　　I bought a Chinese-English Dictionary.

东

dōng

(east)

| 一 | 七 | 车 | 东 | 东 |

在甲骨文里像一件用绳绑着的行李（），有物件的意思，后来才渐渐被用来指示方向。所以，中国人用"东西"这个词来形容物件，正是这个字的本意。

The character 东 in the oracle bones looks like a big bag with its both ends tied ( ), so the original meaning should be 东西 (东西dōng xi: thing). As the character developed and people could no longer discern the original form of "bag", the character also came to mean "the east".

【部首】Radical   一(horizontal line)

【同部首字】Characters under the radical
    万(ten thousand), 不(no), 可(can)

【词语】Words and phrases

东北	dōngběi	northeast
东方	dōngfāng	the east
东风	dōngfēng	east wind
东汉	Dōnghàn	the Eastern Han Dynasty
东南亚	Dōngnán Yà	the Southeast Asia
东欧	Dōng Ōu	Eastern Europe
东西	dōngxi	thing

东奔西跑

    dōng bēn xī pǎo

      run around here and there

东风浩荡

    dōng fēng hào dàng

      The east wind blows with mighty power.

东拉西扯

    dōng lā xī chě

      talk at random

东邻西舍

    dōng lín xī shè

      next door neighbours

【例句】 Example

    他住在东海岸地区。

      tā zhù zài dōng hǎi àn dì qū

        He lives on the east coast.

dōng

(winter)

㇒	夂	夂	冬	冬

　　"冬"像一条头尾都绑上结的线，有"事情已完结"的意思。后来代表"雪"（仌）的符号加在（夂）下面，就变成了后来的"冬"（冬）。冬季是一年四季中最后的一个季节。我们仍可以从有些字中发现"冬"的原意，"纟"＋"冬"构成的"终"意思是"结束"。

　　Originally this character pictured a thread of silk which was knotted at both ends. It was used to indicate that a thing or an incident had come to an end, and it also implied the season at the end of the year. The sign (仌)which means "snow", was added to (夂). Therefore (冬) which later developed into 冬, came to mean winter, the last season of the year. You can still find traces of the original meaning: when the silk radical 纟 is added to 冬 it becomes 终 which means "the end".

【部首】Radical　　夂(tap)

【同部首字】Characters under the radical
　　务(task)，各(each)，条(strip)

【词语】Words and phrases

冬菇	dōnggū	winter mushrooms
冬瓜	dōngguā	wax gourd
冬季	dōngjì	winter(season)
冬天	dōngtiān	winter

冬衣	dōngyī	winter clothes
冬至	dōngzhì	the Winter Solstice (the 22nd solar term)
冬装	dōngzhuāng	winter dress

冬暖夏凉

    dōng nuǎn xià liáng

        cool in summer and warm in winter

冬去春来

    dōng qù chūn lái

        Spring follows winter.

冬夏常青

    dōng xià cháng qīng

        to remain green throughout the year

冬春之交

    dōng chūn zhī jiāo

        at the end of winter and the beginning of spring

【例句】Example

    你的生日在冬天。

        nǐ de shēng rì zài dōng tiān

            Your birthday comes in winter.

多

duō

(many)

ノ	ク	タ	タ	多	多

　　"多"字原来是两块肉（夕）相叠而成，表示"多"的意思，后来简省作两个"夕"。"夕"指夜晚，每天都有，从不间断，因此不断重复的夜晚就有"多"的意思了。

This is an ideogram. It is formed by two 夕, one on top of the other. It signifies that days and nights are changing forever. This meaning then implied the idea of 多, "a lot".

The original meaning of 多 was an antonym of 少 "a little". Later, another meaning was added, which is "more". In Chinese, "two hundred more" means "more than two hundred".

【部首】Radical　　　夕(night)

【同部首字】Characters under the radical

　　外(outside)，岁(age)，名(name)

【词语】Words and phrases

多边	duōbiān	multilateral
多变	duōbiàn	changeable
多病	duōbìng	susceptible to diseases
多寡	duōguǎ	number
多亏	duōkuī	thanks to

多才多艺

    duō cái duō yì

        versatile

多愁善感

    duō chóu shàn gǎn

        sentimental

多如牛毛

    duō rú niú máo

        countless

多灾多难

    duō zāi duō nàn

        be dogged by bad luck

多劳多得

    duō láo duō dé

        more pay for more work

多谋善断

    duō móu shàn duàn

        resourceful and decisive

           i.e., sagacious and resolute

【例句】Example

    多亏你的帮助。

        duō kuī nǐ de bāng zhù

           Thanks to your help.

耳

ěr

(ear)

一	厂	丌	开	耳	耳

　　"耳" 字的最初形象，就像人的耳朵结构（𦘎），分外耳、中耳和内耳三部分。它是人体的听觉器官，演变至现在为止，这个字看起来仍然有点像耳朵呢。

The original character of 耳 "ear" just took the form of a person's ear, placing particular emphasis on the outer ear.

【部首】Radical　　耳(ear)

【同部首字】Characters under the radical
　　　聪(clever)，取(take)，职(duty)

【词语】Words and phrases

耳朵	ěrduo	ear
耳光	ěrguāng	a slap on the face
耳环	ěrhuán	earrings
耳机	ěrjī	earphone
耳鸣	ěrmíng	tinnitus
耳目	ěrmù	what one sees and hears
耳塞	ěrsāi	earplug
耳语	ěryǔ	whisper
耳坠	ěrzhuì	eardrop

耳目一新

ěr mù yì xīn

to find everything fresh and new

耳聪目明

ěr cōng mù míng

have good ears and eyes

i.e., have a clear understanding

耳濡目染

ěr rú mù rǎn

ears soaked and eyes dyed

i.e., be imperceptibly influenced by what one constantly sees and hears

耳熟能详

ěr shú néng xiáng

What has been well-heard can be repeated in detail.

i.e., have heard many times

耳闻不如眼见

ěr wén bù rú yǎn jiàn

Hearsay is not equal to observation.

【例句】Example

不管我说什么，他总是把我的话当耳边风。

bù guǎn wǒ shuō shén me, tā zǒng shì bǎ wǒ de huà dāng ěr biān fēng

Anything I told him went in at one ear and out the other.

分

fēn

(cut)

ノ	八	分	分

　　这个字由"八"字和"刀"字组成，刀子是分割物体的工具，那当然就是指区分、划分了；而"八"字本来也有同样的意思。这个字的含义很多，可以组成很多词语。

　　分 is comprised of two parts: the lower part is a 刀 "knife" which means "to cut"; the upper part is 八 which means something being separated. The idea of this character is to cut something with a knife — which signifies "to separate". From this, the meaning was extended to 分辨(fēnbiàn: to distinguish), and "branch" (of an organization, as in 分店 (fēndiàn: branch of a shop).

【部首】Radical　　　刀(knife)

【同部首字】Characters under the radical
　　切(cut)，召(call together)，初(early, first)

【词语】Words and phrases

分别	fēnbié	part; difference; separately
分布	fēnbù	be distributed
分担	fēndān	share responsibility
分割	fēngē	cut apart
分工	fēngōng	divide the work
分行	fēnháng	branch (of a bank)

| 分机 | fēnjī | extension (telephone) |
| 分居 | fēnjū | (of a couple or members of a family) live apart |

分崩离析

fēn bēng lí xī

fall apart (into pieces)

分辨是非

fēn biàn shì fēi

distinguish between right and wrong

分道扬镳

fēn dào yáng biāo

each going his own way

分工合作

fēn gōng hé zuò

share out the work and cooperate with one another

分身乏术

fēn shēn fá shù

unable to be in two places at the same time

分文不值

fēn wén bù zhí

not worth a cent

【例句】Example

我们对这件事要一分为二来看。

wǒ mén duì zhè jiàn shì yào yì fēn wéi èr lái kàn

We should face this problem (matter) adopting a one-divided-into-two attitude.

夫

fū

(man; husband)

一 二 𡗗 夫

　　古时，一个男孩子到了二十岁，就要用发簪把头发束起来，还要戴上一顶帽子，表示已是成年人，成年后的男子称"夫"。"夫"字还包含着受别人尊敬的意思。

夫 is formed by adding a horizonal stroke above "person" (人), yet this horizonal stroke does not mean "head of the person". Rather, it means the hairpin in a man's hair. In ancient times, when a boy reached the age of 20, he had to bind his hair with a hairpin in a ritual initation, to be considered a grown up man. Therefore, the hairpin is the sign of "a grown up man", and this is also the original meaning of 夫.

【部首】Radical　　　—(horizontal line)

【同部首字】Characters under the radical
　　可(approve)，巫(witch)，末(end, tip)

【词语】Words and phrases

夫妇	fūfù	husband and wife
夫妻	fūqī	husband and wife
夫权	fūquán	authority of the husband
夫人	fūrén	lady; Madame; Mrs.
夫子	fūzǐ	an ancient form of address to a Confucian scholar or to a master by his disciples

懦夫	nuòfū	coward
农夫	nóngfū	farmer
情夫	qíngfū	lover
丈夫	zhàngfu	husband

夫唱妇随

fū chàng fù suí

the husband singing, the wife accompanying

i.e., domestic harmony

夫妇之道

fū fù zhī dào

the proper relations between husband and wife

夫妻无隔夜之仇

fū qī wú gé yè zhī chóu

There is no overnight hatred between man and wife.

【例句】 Example

你认为一夫一妻制怎么样?

nǐ rèn wéi yì fū yì qī zhì zěn me yàng

What do you think of the system of monogamy?

fù

(married woman)

原先这字是由"女"（）字和"帚"（）字组成的，就像手持着扫帚的妇女留在家做家务的模样。"妇"（）当时就是指在家从事家务劳动的女人。

From early inscriptions of this character found on oracle bones, we can see that on the left half of the pictograph there is something like a broom or duster (𝄞), while the right half derives from the character for woman (𝄞). The idea thereby expressed is that a woman with a broom or duster in hand is a married woman.

【部首】Radical   女(female)

【同部首字】Characters under the radical
　　好(good)，妈(mum)，奴(slave)

【词语】Words and phrases

夫妇	fūfù	husband and wife
妇女	fùnǚ	woman
妇人	fùrén	married woman
妇幼	fùyòu	women and children
少妇	shàofù	young married woman

妇人之仁

    fù rén zhī rén

      a woman's kindheartedness

妇道人家

    fù dào rén jiā

      women; womenfolk

妇孺皆知

    fù rú jiē zhī

      even women and children all know

妇人之见

    fù rén zhī jiàn

      views of a woman

        i.e., short sighted or worthless views, not to be taken seriously

【例句】Example

    妇女能顶半边天。

      fù nǚ néng dǐng bàn biān tiān

        Women can support half of heaven.

甘

gān

(sweet; pleasant)

一　十　廿　廿　甘

古代的"甘"字是一个咬着东西的口（廿），美味或鲜甜的东西谁不爱吃？人们爱把美味的食物放在口中慢慢咀嚼和品尝，所以它后来就用来形容一些使人感觉美好的东西。"甘"还引申为"情愿，愿意"。

The pictograph for 甘 is a mouth with a line inside (廿), representing food. Because the food has not been swallowed, but has been kept in the mouth, we know that it must taste good, or sweet. 甘 is also extended to mean " be perfectly happy to".

【部首】Radical　　　一(horizontal line)

【同部首字】Characters under the radical

不(no)，可(can)，丽(pretty)

【词语】Words and phrases

甘苦	gānkǔ	sweetness and bitterness
甘露	gānlù	sweet dew
甘泉	gānquán	fresh spring
甘心	gānxīn	willingly
甘休	gānxiū	be willingly to give up
甘愿	gānyuàn	willingly; readily

甘拜下风

> gān bài xià fēng
>
> > candidly admit defeat

甘瓜苦蒂

> gān guā kǔ dì
>
> > The melon is sweet but the stalk is bitter.

甘棠遗爱

> gān táng yí ài
>
> > sweet memories left behind by a virtuous and capable official

甘心情愿

> gān xīn qíng yuàn
>
> > be perfectly willing

甘言悦耳

> gān yán yuè ěr
>
> > Sweet words are pleasant to the ear.

【例句】 Example

> 他们同甘共苦，心心相印。
>
> > tā mén tóng gān gòng kǔ, xīn xīn xiāng yìn
> >
> > > They shared joys and sorrows, and were kindred spirits.

gāo

(high)

`	亠	宀	亠	古	亠	高	高	高	高

甲骨文里的"高"字（），像一幢多层建筑物，所以有高耸的意思。你看它的形状像不像一座塔？

高 is an adjective, which makes it very difficult to depict. Therefore ancient Chinese used "high fixtures" to represent the idea. In the oracle bones, ( ) depicted a multi-story building, and thus represented the idea of "high".

【部首】Radical 　　亠(above)

【同部首字】Characters under the radical
京(capital of a country)，亮(bright)，市(city)

【词语】 Words and phrases

高矮	gāo'ǎi	height
高潮	gāocháo	high tide
高大	gāodà	tall and big
高度	gāodù	altitude
高贵	gāoguì	noble
高级	gāojí	senior
高温	gāowēn	high temperature

高高在上

　　　gāo gāo zài shàng

　　　　stand high above masses

高官厚禄

　　　gāo guān hòu lù

　　　　high position and handsome salary

高不可攀

　　　gāo bù kě pān

　　　　too high to reach

高不成，低不就

　　　gāo bù chéng, dī bú jiù

　　　　be unfit for a higher post but unwilling to take a lower one

高枕无忧

　　　gāo zhěn wú yōu

　　　　shake up the pillow and have a good sleep

【例句】 Example

　　你的儿子长得很高。

　　　nǐ de ér zǐ zhǎng de hěn gāo

　　　　Your son is very tall.

gōng

(work; labour)

一	丁	工

甲骨文的"工"，就像是古代工匠用的尺子。既然这样，当然就是"工人"、"工作"的意思。

工 is a pictograph. The form of the character on oracle bones seems like a carpenter's square or a ruler. The original meaning for this character is a carpenter's square.

【部首】Radical   工(work)

【同部首字】Characters under the radical
左(left)，巧(skilful)，差(bad)

【词语】 Words and phrases

工厂	gōngchǎng	factory
工程	gōngchéng	engineering; project
工地	gōngdì	building site
工夫	gōngfu	time; skill
工会	gōnghuì	labour union
工匠	gōngjiàng	craftsman
工人	gōngrén	worker
工商业	gōngshāngyè	industry and commerce
工作	gōngzuò	work; job

工力悉敌

    gōng lì xī dí

      be a match for each other in skill

工力深厚

    gōng lì shēn hòu

      remarkable craftsmanship

工诗善画

    gōng shī shàn huà

      be well versed in painting and poetry

工欲善其事，必先利其器

    gōng yù shàn qí shì, bì xiān lì qí qì

      A workman must first sharpen his tools if he wishes to do his work well.

        i.e., Good tools are prerequisite to a successful job.

【例句】 Example

    工作之余，我喜欢运动。

    gōng zuò zhī yú, wǒ xǐ huān yùn dòng

      I like sports after work.

古

gǔ

(ancient; old)

一 十 十 古 古

　　"十" 和 "口" 加起来就得出了 "古" 字，要是一个人有十个口，真吓人。以前资讯传递很落后，一些有价值的事情都是通过别人的口而世代相传，所以就有了这么多的口了。它还有 "古老"、"陈旧" 的意思。

　　It's a combination of 十 "ten" and 口 "mouth", which means there are many mouths. This implies words and wisdom being passed orally over generations and thus the meaning of "old" and "ancient" is derived.

【部首】 Radical 　　口(mouth)

【同部首字】 Characters under the radical
　　召(summon)，叫(call)，吃(eat)

【词语】 Words and phrases

古板	gǔbǎn	old fashioned and inflexible
古代	gǔdài	ancient times; antiquity
古典	gǔdiǎn	classical allusion; classical
古都	gǔdū	ancient capital
古怪	gǔguài	odd; strange
古迹	gǔjì	historical site
古籍	gǔjí	ancient books

古老	gǔlǎo	ancient; age-old
古人	gǔrén	the ancients
古文	gǔwén	prose written in classical literary style

古今中外

    gǔ jīn zhōng wài

        ancient and modern, Chinese and foreign

古色古香

    gǔ sè gǔ xiāng

        antique; quaint

古往今来

    gǔ wǎng jīn lái

        through the ages

古为今用

    gǔ wéi jīn yòng

        make the past serve the present

古道热肠

    gǔ dào rè cháng

        considerate and warmhearted

           i.e., sympathetic

【例句】 Example

    您喜欢这幅古画吗?

        nín xǐ huān zhè fù gǔ huà ma

           Do you like this ancient painting?

光

guāng

(brightness; light; glory)

一	丨	丷	丷	产	光

"光"（）字分上下两部分：一个跪着的人（ ）的头顶上有一团火（ ），这清楚地告诉我们：火能带给人们光明。

We can see that the lower part of this character represents a person ( ) kneeling towards the right; above this person is a fire illuminating the scene ( ). This clearly conveys the idea that it was fire that brought light to mankind, which then lead the way to civilization.

【部首】 Radical　　　儿(son)

【同部首字】 Characters under the radical
兄(elder brother)，先(first)，克(overcome)

【词语】 Words and phrases

光彩	guāngcǎi	lustre; splendour
光华	guānghuá	brilliance; splendour
光环	guānghuán	a ring of light
光洁	guāngjié	bright and clean
光临	guānglín	presence (of a guest)
光明	guāngmíng	light
光荣	guāngróng	honour; glory

光明正大

    guāng míng zhèng dà

        open and aboveboard

            i.e., just and honourable

光天化日

    guāng tiān huà rì

        in the light of the day

光阴似箭

    guāng yīn sì jiàn

        time flying like an arrow

光阴荏苒

    guāng yīn rén rǎn

        Time passes very quickly.

光宗耀祖

    guāng zōng yào zǔ

        making one's ancestors illustrious

【例句】Example

    儿童是世界的希望之光。

        ér tóng shì shì jiè de xī wàng zhī guāng

        Children are the light of our hope in this world.

hǎo

(good; fine; nice)

| | 乚 | 女 | 女 | 好 | 好 | 好 |

看字形便可猜到是一个抱着孩子、弯腰鞠躬的女人（𡥆）。这女人是小婴儿的妈妈，妈妈疼爱地抱着孩子，多美好啊！

In the oracle bones, the left side of this character shows a kneeling woman holding a baby to her breasts (𡥆). This form of the character thus demonstrates that people in ancient times considered a woman with children to be superior to, and better than, a woman without children.

【部首】 Radical　　女(female)

【同部首字】 Characters under the radical
　　姐(elder sister)，她(she, her)，始(begin)

【词语】 Words and phrases

好吃	hǎochī	good to eat; delicious
好多	hǎoduō	a good many
好感	hǎogǎn	favourable impression
好看	hǎokàn	good looking
好人	hǎorén	good person
好玩儿	hǎowánr	amusing

好事多磨

    hǎo shì duō mó

    The road to happiness is strewn with setbacks.

好景不长

    hǎo jǐng bù cháng

    Good times don't last long.

好了疮疤忘了疼

    hǎo le chuāng bā wàng le téng

    When the wound is healed, one forgets the pain.

好自为之

    hǎo zì wéi zhī

    conduct oneself well

好事不出门，恶事传千里

    hǎo shì bù chū mén, è shì chuán qiān lǐ

    Good deeds are never heard of outside door, but bad deeds are proclaimed for three hundred miles.

【例句】Example

    今天天气真好。

    jīn tiān tiān qì zhēn hǎo

    The weather is really fine today.

火

huǒ

(flame; fire)

丶　丶丶　少　火

你看 "火" 的字形（）像不像一团向高空上升的火？而且里头有火舌在动的模样，现在它旁边的两点就表示火舌，"火" 正是物体燃烧时所产生的火焰。它还可以放在左面或下面用作部首，以 "火" 为部首的字常与 "火"、"热" 或火的功能有关。

火 is a pictographic character. As the oracle bones show, it pictures the shape of a flame rising into the air. 火 is a radical in other Chinese characters (there are three forms of the "fire" radical: one is placed on the left side; the others are written on the bottom as a flattened 火, or as four dots). Chinese characters with this radical mostly have something to do with "fire" or "heat", or the functions of fire.

【部首】 Radical　　　火(fire)

【同部首字】 Characters under the radical
灰(ash)，炒(fry)，灾(disaster)

【词语】 Words and phrases

火把	huǒbǎ	torch
火柴	huǒchái	match
火车	huǒchē	train
火光	huǒguāng	blaze
火海	huǒhǎi	a sea of fire

火花	huǒhuā	spark
火鸡	huǒjī	turkey
火箭	huǒjiàn	rocket
火山	huǒshān	volcano

火上加油

　　huǒ shàng jiā yóu

　　　　add oil to the fire

火烧眉毛

　　huǒ shāo méi máo

　　　　fire burning the eyebrows

　　　　　　i.e., a matter of utmost urgency

火树银花

　　huǒ shù yín huā

　　　　a display of firewoods and a sea of lanterns

　　　　　　i.e., on a festival night

火中取栗

　　huǒ zhōng qǔ lì

　　　　pull sb's chestnuts out of the fire

　　　　　　i.e., be a cat's-paw

【例句】Example

　　不能让小孩子玩儿火!

　　　　bù néng ràng xiǎo hái zǐ wángr huǒ

　　　　　　Don't let children play with fire.

吉

jí

(lucky; auspicious; propitious)

一	十	士	吉	吉	吉

细看，"吉"（⚘）的上部是一件兵器（⚘），下部是用来储存兵器的器皿（⚘）。要是人们不再使用兵器，停止战争，就没有战祸所带来的灾害。没有战争的地方，人们便能过安定、和平的生活，是一件"吉"事。

In the oracle bones, the upper part of this character is like a weapon (⚘) and the lower part is like a utensil (⚘) used to store weapons. The combination of these two implies that when weapons are stored away, they are not being used, so there are fewer wars and less danger.

【部首】 Radical   □(mouth)

【同部首字】 Characters under the radical
　　　吞(swallow)，喝(drink)，呼(breathe)

【词语】 Words and phrases

吉利	jílì	lucky
吉普车	jípǔchē	jeep
吉期	jíqī	wedding day
吉庆	jíqìng	auspicious; propitious
吉他	jítā	guitar
吉祥	jíxiáng	lucky

吉光片羽

    jí guāng piàn yǔ

      a fragment of a highly treasured relic

吉人天相

    jí rén tiān xiàng

      Heaven assists the good.

吉日良辰

    jí rì liáng chén

      an auspicious day

吉祥如意

    jí xiáng rú yì

      May you have good fortunes according to your wishes.

【例句】 Example

    七是我的吉祥数字。

      qī shì wǒ de jí xiáng shù zì

        Seven is my lucky number.

家

jiā

(family; home)

`丶 丷 宀 宀 宁 宁 宇 宇 家 家`

　"家" 的上半部是一间屋 (冂)，屋檐下还有一只猪 (豕)。在中国古代社会里，人们在家里养猪来维持生活。所以，猪和人生活在一起，就代表了 "家" 的概念。当然，现在谁也不在家里养猪了，但可不要忘记猪曾经和我们同住一个屋檐下啊！

　This is an associative character comprised of two parts: the upper portion relates to the meaning of "house" (冂), while below the roof there is a pig (豕). In China, as in many other ancient societies, swine, perhaps the earliest of all domesticated animals, along with dogs, were kept close to home. Therefore, a pig residing in or under a house became, through logical association, a symbol of the family's dwelling place, its "home", and by extension and permutation, the family home became the family itself.

【部首】 Radical　　宀(roof)

【同部首字】 Characters under the radical
　　它(it)，守(guard)，安(safe)

【词语】 Words and phrases

家产	jiāchǎn	family property
家教	jiājiào	family education
家眷	jiājuàn	wife and children
家庭	jiātíng	family

家乡   jiāxiāng   one's native place

家常便饭

    jiā cháng biàn fàn

        homely food

家家户户

    jiā jiā hù hù

        each and every family

家丑不可外扬

    jiā chǒu bù kě wài yáng

        Domestic scandals should not be made public.

家家有本难念的经

    jiā jiā yǒu běn nán niàn de jīng

        Every family has a skeleton in the cupboard.

【例句】 Example

    她爱上了一个不回家的人!

        tā ài shàng le yí gè bù huí jiā de rén

           She fell in love with one who doesn't go home!

见

jiàn

(see)

丨	冂	贝	见

"见"有"看见"、"看到"的意思。甲骨文中的"见"字，是一个跪在地上的人（ ），在他的头上有一只大眼睛（ ），意思是一个人正在用眼睛看东西。

This character in the oracle bones represented a person kneeling on the ground facing right ( ). Above the head of the person was a big eye ( ) which gave the idea of someone watching something.

【部首】Radical   见(see)

【同部首字】Characters under the radical
     观(look at)，觉(feel)，览(view)

【词语】Words and phrases

见报	jiànbào	to appear in the newspaper
见地	jiàndì	insight; judgment
见怪	jiànguài	mind; take offence
见解	jiànjiě	view; opinion
见识	jiànshi	experiences; knowledge
见外	jiànwài	regard sb. as an outsider
见闻	jiànwén	what one sees and hears
见效	jiànxiào	become effective

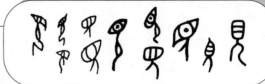

见笑　　　　　jiànxiào　　　　laugh at (me or us)

见风驶舵
> jiàn fēng shǐ duò
>> trim one's sails

见多识广
> jiàn duō shí guǎng
>> experienced and knowledgeable

见仁见智
> jiàn rén jiàn zhì
>> Different people, different views.

见微知著
> jiàn wēi zhī zhù
>> From one small clue one can see what is coming.

见异思迁
> jiàn yì sī qiān
>> change one's mind the moment one sees something new

见义勇为
> jiàn yì yǒng wéi
>> ready to take up arms for a just cause

【例句】Example
> 我见过篮球明星迈克尔·乔丹。
>> wǒ jiàn guò lán qiú míng xīng mài kè ěr qiáo dān
>>> I have met the basketball star Michael Jordan.

交

jiāo

(cross; associate with; hand over)

丶	亠	广	六	亣	交

象形字的"交"，是一个男人交叉着腿站着（），本来有交腿而坐的意思。后来发展出来的意义，又多了"交给"、"交往"等含义。

This pictograph shows a man standing with his legs crossed (　). The original meaning for it was "to cross the feet". Later, it was extended to mean "associate with", as in 交朋友(jiāopéngyou: make friends) or "hand over and take over" as in 交货 (jiāohuò: delivery) etc.

【部首】 Radical 　　亠(above)

【同部首字】 Characters under the radical
　　夜(night)，产(produce)，变(change)

【词语】 Words and phrases

交兵	jiāobīng	be at a war
交叉	jiāochā	intersect; cross
交付	jiāofù	pay
交工	jiāogōng	hand over a completed project
交换	jiāohuàn	exchange
交集	jiāojí	(of different feelings) be mixed
交加	jiāojiā	(of two things) accompany each other

交界	jiāojiè	(of two or more places) have a common boundary
交融	jiāoróng	blend
交通	jiāotōng	traffic
交往	jiāowǎng	association
交易	jiāoyì	trade; deal

交口称誉

jiāo kǒu chēng yù

unanimously praise

交浅言深

jiāo qiǎn yán shēn

give sincere advice to people you hardly know

交相辉映

jiāo xiāng huī yìng

add radiance and beauty to each other

交头接耳

jiāo tóu jiē ěr

speak in each other's ears

水乳交融

shuǐ rǔ jiāo róng

as well blended as milk and water

i.e., be in perfect harmony

【例句】 Example

我来中国交了很多朋友。

wǒ lái zhōng guó jiāo le hěn duō péng yǒu

I have made many friends since I came to China.

jiào

(teach; instruct)

| 一 | 十 | 土 | 少 | 耂 | 耂 | 孝 | 孝 | 孝 | 叛 | 教 |

"教"（教）的右边是一只手握着一根棍子（攵）；而左边是小孩因受体罚后留在头上的疤痕（教）。从这个字看出古时候的教育制度是多么严格。

The original character 教 showed a hand holding a stick on the right side (攵), and on the lower left, a child with some kind of marks on its head from being beaten (教). This shows how education was in the old days, discipline was strict and, as shown in this character, often involved physical punishment.

【部首】Radical   攵(tap)

【同部首字】Characters under the radical
敏(quick)，敬(respect)，数(count)

【词语】Words and phrases

教材	jiàocái	teaching material
教导	jiàodǎo	instruct
教皇	jiàohuáng	pope
教会	jiàohuì	church
教练	jiàoliàn	coach
教室	jiàoshì	classroom
教师	jiàoshī	teacher

教授	jiàoshòu	professor
教学	jiàoxué	education; teaching and studying
教训	jiàoxun	lesson; moral
教育	jiàoyù	education

孺子可教

rú zǐ kě jiào

The boy is worth teaching.

i.e., That's a good boy!

教导有方

jiào dǎo yǒu fāng

skilful in teaching and able to provide guidance

言传身教

yán chuán shēn jiào

teach by precept and example

因材施教

yīn cái shī jiào

educate sb. according to his natural ability

教学相长

jiào xué xiāng zhǎng

Teaching benefits teacher and student alike.

i.e., Both teachers and students make progress by learning from each other.

【例句】 Example

他是一个兼职教师。

tā shì yí gè jiān zhí jiào shī

He is a part-time teacher.

金

jīn

(gold; bronze)

ノ	入	亼	仐	仝	余	金	金

　　最早的"金"（金）字由三部分组成。（▲）是盖子；（±）是地底下的东西；左边的两点（∴）就是地下的矿物，加起来就成了珍贵的地下宝藏。"金"的原意是"金属"。

This character is a combination of an arrowhead (▲) and an ax (±); both of them are made of bronze and the two dots represent bronze ingots (∴). The original meaning of the character is metal.

【部首】 Radical　　金(钅)(metal)

【同部首字】 Characters under the radical
　　钻(drill)，铜(copper)，钟(clock)

【词语】 Words and phrases

金币	jīnbì	gold coin
金刚钻	jīngāngzuàn	diamond
金黄	jīnhuáng	golden yellow
金婚	jīnhūn	golden wedding
金库	jīnkù	national treasury
金器	jīnqì	gold vessel
金钱	jīnqián	money
金融	jīnróng	finance; banking

| | 金鱼 | jīnyú | golden fish |

金科玉律

jīn kē yù lǜ

golden rule and precious precept

金碧辉煌

jīn bì huī huáng

looking splendid in green and gold

金迷纸醉

jīn mí zhǐ zuì

live an extravagant life

金银财宝

jīn yín cái bǎo

gold, silver and other treasures

金屋藏娇

jīn wū cáng jiāo

keep a mistress in a love nest

金玉良言

jīn yù liáng yán

invaluable advice

金玉其外，败絮其中

jīn yù qí wài, bài xù qí zhōng

rubbish coated in gold and jade

金石为开

jīn shí wéi kāi

The utmost sincerity can soften even metal and stone.

i.e., Sincerity can make even metal or stone crack.

【例句】Example

这家商店日进斗金。

zhè jiā shāng diàn rì jìn dǒu jīn

This shop is a regular gold-mine.

kāi

(open)

一	二	于	开

　　最早的"开"字由三部分组成：两边是两扇门，门中间的一横代表门闩，门闩下边是一双手，表示用手去移动门闩。"开"的原意就是"开门"，后来逐渐演变出其他的意思。

The original character 开 was comprised of three parts: on the two sides were the double doors (門); in the middle of the doors there was a horizontal stroke representing the bolt (一); and under the bolt there was a pair of hands, indicating two hands removing the door bolt (鬥). The original meaning of 开 is "to open the door", but later it came to mean "to open" in a general sense.

【部首】Radical　　一(horizontal line)

【同部首字】Characters under the radical
　　干(do)，才(talent)，平(level)

【词语】Words and phrases

开车	kāichē	drive or start a car
开船	kāichuán	set sail
开动	kāidòng	start
开放	kāifàng	be open (to the public)
开花	kāihuā	blossom; bloom
开会	kāihuì	hold a meeting

开课	kāikè	school begins
开口	kāikǒu	open one's mouth; start to talk
开阔	kāikuò	open; wide

开花结果

    kāi huā jié guǒ

        bloom and bear fruits

开卷有益

    kāi juàn yǒu yì

        Reading is always profitable.

开诚相见

    kāi chéng xiāng jiàn

        treat somebody open-heartedly

            i.e., meet or talk in all sincerity

开天辟地

    kāi tiān pì dì

        break fresh ground

开源节流

    kāi yuán jié liú

        to tap new resources of revenue and cut down expenditures

开张大吉

    kāi zhāng dà jí

        Let great prosperity attend the opening of a shop.

【例句】 Example

    客人来了，快去开门!

        kè rén lái le, kuài qù kāi mén

            The guests have come, go to open the door quickly!

看

kàn

(look at; watch; see)

| ㇀ | ⺌ | ㇁ | 手 | 丢 | 看 | 看 | 看 | 看 |

　　"看"字有两部分组成，上半部是一只手（手），下半部是一只眼（目），画的是一个人把手放在眼睛之上，观看四周景物。

This character is a combination of two parts: the upper part is a hand (手), and the lower part is an eye (目), meaning that man raises his hand above his eyes to look into the distance.

【部首】 Radical 　　目(eye)

【同部首字】 Characters under the radical
　　眼(eye)，盲(blind)，眨(wink)

【词语】 Words and phrases

看病	kànbìng	(of a patient) to see a doctor
看出	kànchū	make out; see
看穿	kànchuān	see through
看待	kàndài	treat; regard
看到	kàndào	catch sight of; see
看得起	kàndeqǐ	think highly of
看法	kànfǎ	view
看齐	kànqí	keep abreast with
看轻	kànqīng	underestimate

看望　　　　　　kànwàng　　　　call on; visit

看不顺眼

　　kàn bú shùn yǎn

　　　　to one's dislike

看菜吃饭，量体裁衣

　　kàn cài chī fàn, liáng tǐ cái yī

　　　　Fit one's appetite to the food served, and one's clothing to the figure.

　　　　　　i.e., adapt oneself to the circumstances

看人嘴脸

　　kàn rén zuǐ liǎn

　　　　live on another's favour

【例句】Example

　　你看过"泰坦尼克"这部电影吗?

　　　　nǐ kàn guò tài tǎn ní kè zhè bù diàn yǐng ma

　　　　　　Have you seen the film *Titanic*?

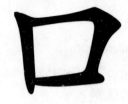

口

kǒu

(mouth)

"口"字在象形字中，画了一张快乐的嘴（ㅂ），这便是"口"的原本意思。口是人用来说话和吃东西的器官，它后来又有了"张开"和"人口"的意思。

This is a pictograph of a mouth with happy corners. The original meaning of 口 is "mouth", and from this meaning it is extended to represent 人口(rén kǒu:"person's mouth"— "population"). "五口之家" (wǔ kǒu zhī jiā) " family of five mouths" means "a family with five persons". In addition, 口 also means "opening".

【部首】Radical   口(mouth)

【同部首字】Characters under the radical
    号(number)，名(name)，味(taste)

【词语】 Words and phrases

口碑	kǒubēi	public praise
口才	kǒucái	eloquence
口袋	kǒudài	pocket
口号	kǒuhào	slogan
口渴	kǒukě	thirsty
口试	kǒushì	oral examination
口味	kǒuwèi	personal taste

□□相传

    kǒu kǒu xiāng chuán

        go from mouth to mouth

□□声声

    kǒu kǒu shēng shēng

        say again and again

□蜜腹剑

    kǒu mì fù jiàn

        honey on the lips and murder in the heart

□是心非

    kǒu shì xīn fēi

        affirm with one's lips but deny in one's heart

□诛笔伐

    kǒu zhū bǐ fá

        condemn both in speech and in writing

□服心不服

    kǒu fú xīn bù fú

        agree in words but not in mind

【例句】 Example

    请你不要口是心非!

        qǐng nǐ bú yào kǒu shì xīn fēi

           Please don't say yes and mean no!

牢

láo

(prison; firm; durable)

丶	丷	宀	宀	宀	宊	牢

　　你看这个字（），很像一只牛被困在围栏里。把牛围起来就可防止牛逃跑，就正如囚犯被困在监牢一样，而且监牢必须要稳固，才可防止囚犯逃走。所以牢就有了"稳固"的含义。

Looking at the original form of this character we can see it looks like an "ox" enclosed in a corral ( ). As the character evolved, a mark was added which represented a big log leaning against the corral gate, so that ox would not be able to run out. In this way, the corral has became more sturdy. So the original meaning for 牢 was "corral for oxen". But the meaning came to indicate also "a place for caging a criminal", like 囚牢 (qiū láo), 监牢 (jiān láo), "prison" or "jail". Since a "prison" or "jail" must be "firm", so 牢 can be used as an adjective as well as a noun.

【部首】Radical　　宀(roof)

【同部首字】Characters under the radical
　　家(family)，富(rich)，宝(treasure)

【词语】Words and phrases

牢固	láogù	firm; secure
牢记	láojì	keep firmly in mind
牢靠	láokào	strong; sturdy

牢牢	láoláo	firmly
牢笼	láolóng	cage; bonds
牢狱	láoyù	prison; jail

牢不可破

　　láo bù kě pò

　　　　unbreakable

牢笼人心

　　láo lóng rén xīn

　　　　captivate the mind of men

牢落不群

　　láo luò bù qún

　　　　keeping oneself aloof

牢愁莫遣

　　láo chóu mò qiǎn

　　　　worried not knowing how to drive away melancholy

【例句】 Example

　　把绳子拴牢。

　　　　bǎ shéng zǐ shuān láo

　　　　　　Tie the rope fast.

lǎo

(old)

| 一 | 十 | 土 | 耂 | 耂 | 老 |

　　甲骨文的"老"字，从侧面看就像一个长发、驼背、手持拐杖的老人（𦒍）。这字是指年纪大的人，七十岁以上便是高龄老人。其他与"老"有关的字，例如孝、长等，都是由这个字变出来的。

The oracle bones picture the character (𦒍) as an old man facing the left, with a hunched back, long hair and a stick in his hand. Other characters relating to "old" or "elders" which are derived from this character include 孝 (xiào:filial piety) and 长 (zhǎng: elder).

【部首】 Radical　　老(old)

【同部首字】 Characters under the radical
　　考(test)，耆(old people)

【词语】 Words and phrases

老板	lǎobǎn	boss
老伴儿	lǎobànr	(of an old married couple) husband or wife
老本	lǎoběn	capital
老成	lǎochéng	experienced; steady
老粗	lǎocū	uneducated person
老家	lǎojiā	native place
老练	lǎoliàn	seasoned; experienced

老脑筋	lǎonǎojīn	old-fashioned(or outmoded)way of thinking
老年	lǎonián	old age
老师	lǎoshī	teacher
老实	lǎoshí	honest; frank
老乡	lǎoxiāng	fellow-townsman

老弱病残

    lǎo ruò bìng cán

        the old, weak, sick and disabled

老生常谈

    lǎo shēng cháng tán

        platitudes; commonplace

老当益壮

    lǎo dāng yì zhuàng

        old but vigorous

老马识途

    lǎo mǎ shí tú

        The old horse knows the way.

老吾老以及人之老

    lǎo wú lǎo yǐ jí rén zhī lǎo

        show respect for one's seniors and for others

老虎屁股摸不得

    lǎo hǔ pì gǔ mō bù dé

        like a tiger whose backside no one dares to touch

老王卖瓜，自卖自夸

    lǎo wáng mài guā, zì mài zì kuā

        Lao Wang the melon-seller praises his own goods.

          i.e., to praise one's own work or wares

老骥伏枥，志在千里

    lǎo jì fú lì, zhì zài qiān lǐ

        An old steed in the stable still aspires to gallop a thousand miles.

          i.e., Old people may still cherish high aspirations.

【例句】Example

    他办事老练。

        tā bàn shì lǎo liàn

        He is experienced and works with a sure hand.

léi

(thunder)

一 冖 冖 币 币 币 币 币 雱 霄 霄 雷 雷

　　最初的"雷"字（）像四个连在一起的鼓，因为雷声响得像鼓声。后来在上面加个"雨"字作部首，本来连在一起的四个鼓亦简化为一个，就成了现在所写的"雷"字。

The ancient form of 雷 (⟨⟩) depicts lightning accompanied by peals of thunder. Because a thunderclap sounds like drumming, it was depicted by four drum heads linked together. Later it was also topped with the radical 雨; the four drum heads were reduced to three, and gradually three were reduced to one, to produce the form we use today.

【部首】Radical　　雨(rain)

【同部首字】Characters under the radical
　　雪(snow)，雹(hail)，零(zero)

【词语】Words and phrases

雷暴	léibào	thunderstorm
雷达	léidá	radar
雷电	léidiàn	thunder and lightning
雷动	léidòng	thunderous
雷声	léishēng	thunderclap
雷阵雨	léizhènyǔ	thunder shower

雷打不动

    léi dǎ bú dòng

       unshakable

雷厉风行

    léi lì fēng xíng

       vigorously and speedily

雷霆万钧

    léi tíng wàn jūn

       as powerful as a thunderbolt

雷声大，雨点小

    léi shēng dà, yǔ diǎn xiǎo

       loud thunder but small raindrops

          i.e., much said but little done

【例句】 Example

    气象预报今天会有雷雨。

       qì xiàng yù bào jīn tiān huì yǒu léi yǔ

       The weather forecast reports that there will be thunder and shower today.

力

lì

(power; strength)

フ	力

　　在甲骨文里，"力"字就像古时的犁（），而象形字的"力"也可以用作动词"耕"的意思。这个字告诉我们：农耕是需要力气的！

　　From the oracle bones we can see that the original form of ( ) is like an ancient plough: the upper part, which curves at the bottom, is the wooden handle of a plough, and the lower part is its iron head. 力 is a pictograph of a plough and was used as the verb "to plough a field". Since ploughing the field requires strength, 力 then was used to express the meaning "force", "power" or "strength".

【部首】 Radical　　力(strength)

【同部首字】 Characters under the radical
　　劫(rob)，动(move)，势(trend)

【词语】 Words and phrases

力量	lìliang	physical strength; power; force
力气	lìqi	physical strength; effort
力求	lìqiú	do one's best to
力图	lìtú	try hard to; strive to
力争	lìzhēng	work hard to
人力	rénlì	manpower; labour force

力薄才疏

    lì bó cái shū

       be deficient in strength and ability

力排众议

    lì pái zhòng yì

       reject strongly different opinions

力不从心

    lì bù cóng xīn

       ability not equal to one's ambition

力所能及

    lì suǒ néng jí

       within one's power

力透纸背

    lì tòu zhǐ bèi

       (of poem etc.) profound in conception and succinct in language

力挽狂澜

    lì wǎn kuáng lán

       make vigorous efforts to turn the tide

力争上游

    lì zhēng shàng yóu

       strive for the best

【例句】Example

这件事费了很大的力才做成。

    zhè jiàn shì fèi le hěn dà de lì cái zuò chéng

       This task requires a lot of effort to be done well.

mǎ

(horse)

フ	马	马

象形字中的"马"（）能看到马的特征：身躯跃起、头向上、尾向下，中间还有鬃毛。后来马的特征渐渐消失了，简化成现今的"马"字。

（　）is a pictographic character which depicts a horse with its head upwards, tail downwards and back to the right; it even depicts the hair. But as the character developed it lost these original pictographic features.

【部首】 Radical   马(horse)

【同部首字】 Characters under the radical
驾(drive)，驰(gallop)，驶(sail, drive)

【词语】 Words and phrases

马鞭	mǎbiān	horsewhip
马车	mǎchē	cart
马达	mǎdá	motor
马大哈	mǎdàhā	a careless person
马队	mǎduì	a team of horses
马夫	mǎfū	groom
马虎	mǎhu	careless
马铃薯	mǎlíngshǔ	potato

| 马路 | mǎlù | road; avenue |
| 马上 | mǎshàng | at once |

马不停蹄

    mǎ bù tíng tí

        The horse gallops on without stopping.

            i.e., non stop

马首是瞻

    mǎ shǒu shì zhān

        take the head of the general's horse as guide

            i.e., follow sb's lead

马仰人翻

    mǎ yǎng rén fān

        men and horses thrown off their feet

            i.e., to be turned upside-down

马革裹尸

    mǎ gé guǒ shī

        be wrapped in a horse's hide after death

            i.e., die on the battlefield

马屁拍到马腿上

    mǎ pì pāi dào mǎ tuǐ shàng

        flatter sb. the wrong way

【例句】Example

    你马上就走吗?

        nǐ mǎ shàng jiù zǒu ma

            Are you leaving right away?

mǎi

(buy)

| ㇇ | ㇇ | ㇗ | 三 | 买 | 买 |

　　最初的"买"字，上面是一个用来盛载贝壳类海产的渔网（网），下面是贝壳（贝），有"交易"和"购买"的意思。以贝字作部首，通常是和金钱有关的，它提醒你：以前的人是用贝壳来做钱币的！

　　This is an associative compound character which originally combined the symbol for "net" ( ), meaning "dredge", with a "shellfish" ( ), meaning "merchandise", indicating to "purchase" or "buy" the merchandise.

【部首】Radical　　　㇇(one)

【同部首字】Characters under the radical
　　予(give)，了(end)，承(bear)

【词语】Words and phrases

买办	mǎibàn	comprador
买方	mǎifāng	the buying party
买价	mǎijià	buying price
买卖	mǎimài	buying and selling; commerce
买通	mǎitōng	to bribe; buy over
买主	mǎizhǔ	buyer

买空卖空

  mǎi kōng mài kōng

    speculate on the rise and fall of prices

买卖公平

  mǎi mài gōng píng

    to buy and sell at reasonable prices

买笑追欢

  mǎi xiào zhuī huān

    to buy laughter and seek pleasure

买椟还珠

  mǎi dú huán zhū

    keep the glittering casket and give back the pearls to the seller

      i.e., choose the wrong thing

【例句】Example

  我在北京买了很多东西。

    wǒ zài běi jīng mǎi le hěn duō dōng xī

      I bought a lot of things in Beijing.

眉

méi

(eyebrow)

| ⊐ | ⊐ | ⊐ | 尸 | 尸 | 尸 | 尸 | 眉 | 眉 |

这个字是象形字的最佳例子。看，（〝〝）就在眼睛（〇）的上面，不是眉毛是什么？

This is a very good example of pictogram. The (〝〝) on top of eye (〇) represents the eyebrows.

【部首】Radical　　目(eye)

【同部首字】Characters under the radical
　　瞎(blind)，眼(eye)，盼(look forward to)

【词语】Words and phrases

眉笔	méibǐ	eyebrow pencil
眉毛	méimao	eyebrow; brow
眉目	méimù	features; looks; prospect of a solution
眉批	méipī	notes and commentary
眉梢	méishāo	the tip of the brow
眉头	méitóu	brows
眉心	méixīn	between the eyebrows
眉宇	méiyǔ	forehead

眉开眼笑

    méi kāi yǎn xiào

        be all smiles

            i.e.,beam with joy

眉来眼去

    méi lái yǎn qù

        make eyes at each other

眉飞色舞

    méi fēi sè wǔ

        with dancing eyebrows and radiant face

            i.e., enraptured

眉清目秀

    méi qīng mù xiù

        have delicate features

【例句】Example

    他听到这个消息，高兴得眉飞色舞。

        tā tīng dào zhè gè xiāo xī, gāo xìng de méi fēi sè wǔ

        When he heard this news, he was delighted with dancing eyebrows and radiant face.

门

mén

(door; gate)

`	冂	门

　　相信你一看这个图形（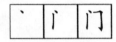）便认出它是"门"字，因为它画出了两扇相对的门，这是古旧建筑用的木板门。还有，通常用"门"作部首的字，都与"门"、"闸"等东西有关，很易认。

　　门 is a pictograph showing a set of double doors (門). 门 is also a radical; the characters with this radical usually have something to do with the meaning of "door" or "gate".

【部首】 Radical　　门(door)

【同部首字】 Characters under the radical

　　阅(read)，阔(wide)，阁(pavilion)

【词语】 Words and phrases

门第	méndì	family status
门户	ménhù	door; faction
门警	ménjǐng	police guard at an entrance
门径	ménjìng	access; key
门槛	ménkǎn	threshold
门口	ménkǒu	entrance; doorway
门框	ménkuàng	door-frame
门廊	ménláng	porch

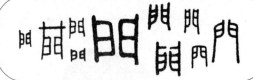

门帘	ménlián	door curtain
门面	ménmiàn	the facade of a shop
门牌	ménpái	(house) number plate
门徒	méntú	disciple; follower
门诊	ménzhěn	outpatient service

门户之见

mén hù zhī jiàn

   sectarianism

门禁森严

mén jìn sēn yán

   with the entrances heavily guarded

门庭若市

mén tíng ruò shì

   The courtyard is like a market fair.

      i.e., having many visitors

门当户对

mén dāng hù duì

   be well-matched in social and economic status (for marriage)

【例句】 Example

今天晚上七点我在大学门口等你。

   jīn tiān wǎn shàng qī diǎn wǒ zài dà xué mén kǒu děng nǐ

   I'll wait for you at seven o'clock at the entrance of the university.

miàn

(face)

一 丆 丆 丙 而 而 而 面 面

古时的"面"字，把人的面部轮廓勾画出来（）：头发、眼睛、鼻子、嘴巴。后来再加上脸，就变成现在的"面"字。

The original character of 面 shows the attempt to depict a man's face.

【部首】Radical　　一(horizontal line)

【同部首字】Characters under the radical
　　万(ten thousand)，天(sky)

【词语】Words and phrases
面对	miànduì	confront; to face
面积	miànji	area
面颊	miànjiá	cheek
面具	miànjù	mask
面貌	miànmào	looks; features
面色	miànsè	complexion
面熟	miànshóu	look familiar
面谈	miàntán	speak to somebody face to face
面子	miànzi	reputation

面不改色

    miàn bù gǎi sè

       not change colour

          i.e., remain calm

面红耳赤

    miàn hóng ěr chì

       be red in the face

面面俱到

    miàn miàn jù dào

       attend to each and every aspect of a matter

面和心不和

    miàn hé xīn bù hé

       remain friendly in appearance but estranged at heart

【例句】Example

    我们面对困难决不退缩。

      wǒ mén miàn duì kùn nán jué bú tuì suō

        We will never flinch from difficulties.

鸣

míng

(of a bird) to sing

丶	丷	口	口′	吖	吗	鸣	鸣

　　"鸣"字的组成很有趣：右面是一只伸长了脖子在歌唱的小鸟；左面是一个唱歌的口。它本来是指"鸟的歌唱"，后来就用来指所有动物的叫声，像"蝉鸣"，"虫鸣"等。现在连人们争辩时所发出的声音也叫"鸣"了，"百家争鸣"就是最好的例子。

　　鸣 is comprised of two pictographs: from the inscriptions on oracle bones, we can see clearly on the right side a bird stretching out its neck with its mouth open in song, and on the left side, a "mouth" radical which also suggests singing. So the original meaning for 鸣 is "bird sings". Later, from this meaning it was extended to include the sound made by any animal or insect, like 鹿鸣 "lù míng", 虫鸣 "chóng míng": It has even come to be used to describe human's debating as in the saying 百家争鸣 (bǎi jiā zhēng míng: a hundred schools of thought contend.)

【部首】 Radical　　　□(mouth)

【同部首字】Characters under the radical
　　喊(shout)，吻(kiss)，听(listen)

【词语】 Words and phrases

耳鸣	ěrmíng	ringing in the ears
鸡鸣	jīmíng	the crow of a cock
鸣笛	míngdí	whistle

鸣鼓	mínggǔ	beat a drum
鸣炮	míngpào	fire a shot
鸣枪	míngqiāng	fire a gun

鸣鼓而攻

    míng gǔ ér gōng

        beat the drum and launch the attack

            i.e., attack somebody publicly

鸣金收兵

    míng jīn shōu bīng

        beat the gong to call back the troops

            i.e., call off the battle

鸣锣开道

    míng luó kāi dào

        beat the gong to clear the way

            i.e., clear the way for something

鸣冤叫屈

    míng yuān jiào qū

        complain and call for redress

            i.e., voice one's discontent

不鸣则已，一鸣惊人

    bú míng zé yǐ, yì míng jīng rén

        not speak unless able to say something sensational

【例句】Example

    他这个人不鸣则已，一鸣惊人。

        tā zhè gè rén bù míng zé yǐ, yì míng jīng rén

            He is a someone who does not speak unless able to say something sensational.

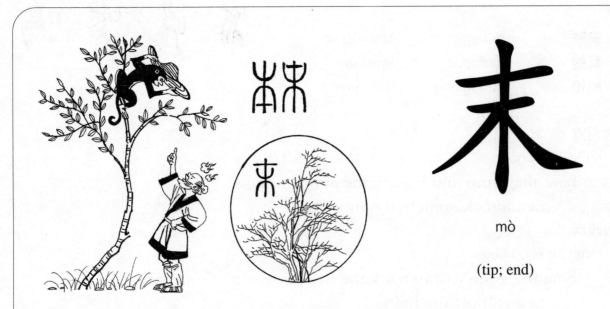

末

mò

(tip; end)

一 二 㐁 才 末

　　"末"是在木（朩）的树顶上加上一横（朩），就是树的上端、树梢了，用来形容事物的"末端"或"尖端"，后来指"不重要的事情"。成语"本末倒置"说的就是人们把事物的轻重次序颠倒过来的意思。

On the contrary of 本, 末 is constructed by adding a short stroke on the upper part of (朩) indicating the tip of the tree (朩). So the original meaning of 末 is "tip" or "end", and it is also extended for the meaning of the things that is not important.

【部首】Radical　　木(tree)

【同部首字】Characters under the radical
　　枕(pillow), 树(tree), 村(village)

【词语】Words and phrases

末代	mòdài	the last reign of a dynasty
末了	mòliǎo	in the end; last
末路	mòlù	deadend
末年	mònián	last years of a dynasty or reign
末期	mòqī	last phase
末日	mòrì	doomsday
末尾	mòwěi	end

末路穷途

    mò lù qióng tú

      be driven into an impasse

舍本逐末

    shě běn zhú mò

      to grasp the shadow instead of the essence

末路之难

    mò lù zhī nán

      the arduousness of the last section of the journey

        i.e., The nearer to success, the more arduous.

本末倒置

    běn mò dào zhì

      take the branch for the root

        i.e., put the cart before the horse

秋毫之末

    qiū háo zhī mò

      the tip of an animal's autumn hair

【例句】Example

    今天是本学期的最末一天。

      jīn tiān shì běn xué qī de zuì mò yì tiān

        Today is the last day of this term.

木

mù

(tree; wood)

一 十 才 木

象形字的木（ ），上面似树枝（ ），下面似树根（ ），就是指树木、木材。

As we can see, this character is a pictograph of a tree ( ). The upper part is the treetop with its branches ( ), and the lower part is the roots ( ). The original meaning of this character is " tree", and it also stands for "wood" in general.

【部首】Radical　　木(tree)

【同部首字】Characters under the radical

杆(pole)，森(forest)，杏(apricot)

【词语】Words and phrases

木材	mùcái	timber
木匠	mùjiang	carpenter
木结构	mùjiégòu	timber structure
木屋	mùwū	log cabin
木箱	mùxiāng	wooden box
木星	mùxīng	Jupiter

木本水源

    mù běn shuǐ yuán

       the root of wood and the source of water

          i.e., the foundation or cause of things

木头木脑

    mù tóu mù nǎo

       wooden-headed

木已成舟

    mù yǐ chéng zhōu

       The wood is already made into a boat.

          i.e., What is done cannot be undone.

【例句】 Example

    独木不成林，人多力量大。

       dú mù bù chéng lín, rén duō lì liàng dà

          A single tree does not make a forest, just as more people have more strength.

mù

(eye)

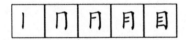

　　"目"字最早的时候，很像一只"眼睛"（）。后来眼睛直立了起来，使它原本的形状消失，变成了现在的"目"字，它中间的两画表示了眼珠的轮廓。你现在看这个字，仍然想像得到它原来的形状吧！

　　The drawing of (⏜) looks just like a real eye, and the original meaning of this character is precisely that. Later the curve indicating the iris of the eye was flattened, and the eye was turned to stand on its end before finally losing the shape of an eye.

【部首】Radical　　目(eye)

【同部首字】Characters under the radical
　　盯(stare)，睡(sleep)，盼(look forward to)

【词语】Words and phrases

目标	mùbiāo	objective; aim
目的	mùdi	purpose
目睹	mùdǔ	see with one's eyes
目光	mùguāng	sight
目击	mùjī	see with one's own eyes
目录	mùlù	catalogue
目前	mùqián	at present

| 目送 | mùsòng | watch somebody go |
| 目眩 | mùxuàn | dizzy |

目不交睫

    mù bù jiāo jié

        not sleep at all

目不暇接

    mù bù xiá jiē

        The eye cannot take it all in.

目不斜视

    mù bù xié shì

        not look sideways

目瞪口呆

    mù dèng kǒu dāi

        be stunned

            i.e., speechless

目光如豆

    mù guāng rú dòu

        with a vision as large as a bean

            i.e., extremely short-sighted

目空一切

    mù kōng yí qiè

        look down upon everything

耳濡目染

    ěr rú mù rǎn

        eyes dyed and ears soaked

            i.e., be imperceptibly influenced by what one constantly sees and hears

目中无人

    mù zhōng wú rén

        consider everyone beneath one's notice

【例句】 Example

    他目中无人，很没礼貌。

        tā mù zhōng wú rén, hěn méi lǐ mào

            He is very impolite and consider everyone beneath his notice.

男

nán

(man; male)

| 丶 | 冂 | 曰 | 囲 | 田 | 罗 | 男 |

这字古时由两部分组成：左面是一块田（囲），右面是一个像犁的工具（丿）。因为在古时候，下田耕种的工作主要由男人负责。

The original character of 男 was a combination of two parts: the left side was a field (囲), and the right side was a plough-like tool (丿). As ploughing the field was men's work in ancient times, the original meaning of 男 is "the strength in the field" or "man".

【部首】Radical   田(field)

【同部首字】Characters under the radical
    界(boundary)，畏(fear)，申(apply)

【词语】Words and phrases
男女	nánnǚ	man and woman
男朋友	nánpéngyǒu	boy friend
男人	nánrén	man
男性	nánxìng	male
男子汉	nánzǐhàn	man; hero

男耕女织

    nán gēng nǚ zhī

        divisions of labour

男男女女

    nán nán nǚ nǚ

        men and women

男女平等

    nán nǚ píng děng

        equality of men and women

男女授受不亲

    nán nǚ shòu shòu bù qīn

        It is improper for men and women to touch each other's hand in
        passing objects.

【例句】Example

    男孩子不一定比女孩子顽皮。

        nán hái zǐ bù yí dìng bǐ nǚ hái zǐ wán pí

        Boys are not surely more naughty than girls.

niǎo

(bird)

| ´ | ㄅ | ㄅ | 鸟 | 鸟 |

这个字（）把鸟的外貌特征全部表现出来：头部、翅膀、爪，后来又加上眼睛，相信大家一看便会认出是"鸟"。

鸟 is a pictograph of a bird with a head, wings, claws, and a tail, which are easily identifiable; later, the eyes were also added.

【部首】Radical   鸟(bird)

【同部首字】Characters under the radical
　　鸭(duck)，鸳鸯(mandarin duck)，鸽(pigeon)

【词语】Words and phrases

鸟瞰	niǎokàn	get a bird's eye view
鸟类	niǎolèi	birds
鸟笼	niǎolóng	birdcage
鸟枪	niǎoqiāng	fowling piece; air gun
鸟兽	niǎoshòu	birds and beasts
鸟嘴	niǎozuǐ	beak; bill

鸟尽弓藏

niǎo jìn gōng cáng

cast aside the bow once the birds are gone

鸟语花香

niǎo yǔ huā xiāng

birds sing and flowers give forth their fragrance

鸟之将死，其鸣也哀

niǎo zhī jiāng sǐ, qí míng yě āi

When a bird is dying its cry is pitiful.

鸟为食亡，人为财死

niǎo wèi shí wáng, rén wèi cái sǐ

Birds die in pursuit of food, and human beings die in pursuit of wealth.

鸟无翅不飞，蛇无头不行

niǎo wú chì bù fēi, shé wú tóu bù xíng

A bird without wings cannot fly and a snake without head cannot crawl.

【例句】Example

我们在飞机上鸟瞰黄河。

wǒ mén zài fēi jī shàng niǎo kàn huáng hé

From the plane we had a bird's eye view of the Yellow River.

牛

niú

(ox; cow; bull)

ノ	┌	二	牛

这字描绘出牛的正面，相信一看这个图形（ψ）你便会猜到它是牛。两边向上的曲线是牛角，牛角下的当然是牛耳，后来牛耳被拉直，就是我们现今所看到的"牛"字。

The original form of this character was the front view of an ox's head (ψ). The two sides of it which curved upwards are the horns of the ox, and the two strokes below the horn stretching out are ears. Later the ears were straightened to be a horizontal stroke and the form of the character became what we see today.

【部首】Radical   牛(ox)

【同部首字】Characters under the radical
      牧(herd)，牲(domestic animal)，特(special)

【词语】Words and phrases

牛犊	niúdú	calf
牛角尖	niújiǎojiān	the tip of a horn
牛劲	niújìn	great strength
牛栏	niúlán	cattle pen
牛毛	niúmáo	ox hair
牛奶	niúnǎi	milk
牛脾气	niúpíqì	stubbornness

牛肉	niúròu	beef
牛童	niútóng	buffalo boy
牛仔裤	niúzǎikù	jeans

牛刀小试

　　niú dāo xiǎo shì

　　　　a master hand's first small display

牛刀割鸡

　　niú dāo gē jī

　　　　kill a chicken with a butcher's big knife

　　　　　　i.e., great talent used in petty things

牛马不如

　　niú mǎ bù rú

　　　　worked even harder than oxen and horses

牛不喝水强按头

　　niú bù hē shuǐ qiáng àn tóu

　　　　force an ox to bend its head to drink

　　　　　　i.e., force someone to do something

牛头不对马嘴

　　niú tóu bú duì mǎ zuǐ

　　　　Horses' jaws don't match cows' heads.

　　　　　　i.e., incongruous

【例句】Example

　　我习惯每天早上喝一杯牛奶。

　　　　wǒ xí guàn měi tiān zǎo shàng hē yì bēi niú nǎi

　　　　　I get used to drinking a cup of milk every morning.

nǚ

(woman; girl)

く	夂	女

　　最早的象形字是把"女"字画成双手放在前面，一副鞠躬的样子（ 𢀖 ）；渐渐地，又把"女"画得像一个跪下的女人，两手交叉放在胸前，这是古代妇女的形象。

In ancient times the position of women was as low as that of slaves, so the earliest known pictographs for woman show her in a bowing position with her arms crossed in front of her body (𢀖). Subsequent developments show her in a kneeling position.

【部首】Radical 　　女(female)

【同部首字】Characters under the radical

好(good)，妈(mother)，要(want)

【词语】Words and phrases

女皇	nǚhuáng	empress
女郎	nǚláng	young woman; maiden
女神	nǚshén	goddess
女士	nǚshì	lady
女巫	nǚwū	witch; sorceress
女主人	nǚzhǔrén	hostess
淑女	shūnǚ	fair lady

女中丈夫

    nǚ zhōng zhàng fū

      as a man amongst the woman folks

女大当嫁

    nǚ dà dāng jià

      A grown-up girl should marry at time.

女大十八变

    nǚ dà shí bā biàn

      A girl changes fast in physical appearance from childhood to adulthood.

女子无才便是德

    nǚ zǐ wú cái biàn shì dé

      An unaccomplished woman should be a virtuous woman.

【例句】 Example

    她是一个独身女子。

      tā shì yí gè dú shēn nǚ zǐ

        She is a single woman.

气

qì

(air; gas)

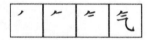

最原始的"气"是由三条横线（三）组成，分别代表三层正向高空上升的云。后来因为它和数字"三"相近，所以就在它头部和尾部都加上曲线（气）。

The original pictograph was of clouds floating in the air. Three horizontal lines showed the layers of the clouds with the middle layer shorter than the other two, implying emptiness (三). To avoid confusion with another character 三 "three", people later gave the top and bottom layers a curly tail (气).

【部首】Radical   气(air)

【同部首字】Characters under the radical
氧(oxygen)，氛(atomsphere)

【词语】Words and phrases

气窗	qìchuāng	transom window
气度	qìdù	tolerance; bearing
气短	qìduǎn	be short of breath
气氛	qìfen	atmosphere
气愤	qìfèn	indignant
气概	qìgài	lofty quality; spirit
气功	qìgōng	a system of deep breathing exercises; *qigong*

气候	qìhou	climate
气呼呼	qìhūhū	in a huff
气节	qìjié	integrity; moral courage
气力	qìlì	effort; energy
气流	qìliú	air current

气急败坏

　　qì jí bài huài

　　　　flustered and exasperated

气势磅礴

　　qì shì páng bó

　　　　of great momentum

气势汹汹

　　qì shì xiōng xiōng

　　　　fierce

气吞山河

　　qì tūn shān hé

　　　　imbued with a spirit that can conquer mountains and rivers

气味相投

　　qì wèi xiāng tóu

　　　　have the same tastes and temperament

【例句】 Example

　　打开窗子透一透气吧!

　　　　dǎ kāi chuāng zǐ tòu yí tòu qì ba

　　　　　　Let's open the window to get some fresh air!

取

qǔ

(take; get)

一	厂	丌	丌	月	耳	耵	取

　　这字的左边是一只耳朵（耳），右边是一只手（又）。为什么会用耳朵和手拼成这个字呢?原来古人会把敌人的左耳割下来，用来向上级领功，所以"取"字本来就是指"割下左耳朵"的意思。

　　取 is an associative compound character. On the left side it is an "ear" (耳) and on the right side a "hand" (又). As in ancient times the war prisoners would have their left ears to be lopped off as testimony to their military exploits, so the original meaning of 取 was "to cut off the left ear"; from this the character was also extended to express the present meaning "take", "get" or "fetch".

【部首】Radical　　　耳(ear)

【同部首字】Characters under the radical
　　　聪(clever)，聋(deaf)，聊(chat)

【词语】Words and phrases

取代	qǔdài	replace
取道	qǔdào	by way of
取得	qǔdé	gain; obtain
取缔	qǔdì	outlaw; ban
取经	qǔjīng	learn from sb. else's experience

取决	qǔjué	depend on
取暖	qǔnuǎn	warm oneself
取胜	qǔshèng	win victory
取消	qǔxiāo	cancel
取笑	qǔxiào	make fun of

舍身取义

　　shě shēn qǔ yì

　　　　sacrifice profit to duty

以貌取人

　　yǐ mào qǔ rén

　　　　to judge people solely by their appearance

取长补短

　　qǔ cháng bǔ duǎn

　　　　learn from others' strong points to offset one's weakness

取之不尽，用之不竭

　　qǔ zhī bú jìn, yòng zhī bù jié

　　　　inexhaustible

取之于民，用之于民

　　qǔ zhī yú mín, yòng zhī yú mín

　　　　What is taken from the people is used for the people.

【例句】 Example

　　我们取道上海前往东京。

　　　　wǒ mén qǔ dào shàng hǎi qián wǎng dōng jīng

　　　　　We go to Tokyo via Shanghai.

去

qù

(go; leave)

| 一 | 十 | 土 | 去 | 去 |

　　甲骨文中，"去"字分为两部分：上半部是一个人（大），下半部是一个口（凵）。古时的人住在洞穴里，从洞穴口离去，就有"离开"的意思。

　　去 was comprised of two parts in the oracle bones: the upper part was originally a person (大), and the lower part was a mouth (凵 or 凵). This indicated that a person had left the mouth of a cave. So the original meaning of 去 was "to leave", but it has also been extended to mean "to go" or "to remove", etc.

【部首】 Radical　　土(earth)

【同部首字】 Characters under the radical
　　地(field)，尘(dust)

【词语】 Words and phrases

去处	qùchù	place to go
去路	qùlù	outlet
去年	qùnián	last year
去世	qùshì	(of grown-up people) die; pass away
去污粉	qùwūfěn	household cleanser
去向	qùxiàng	the direction in which sb. or sth. has gone

去粗取精

　　qù cū qǔ jīng

　　　　discard the dross and select the essential

去伪存真

　　qù wěi cún zhēn

　　　　eliminate the false and retain the true

去恶从善

　　qù è cóng shàn

　　　　exterminate the evil and follow the good

去邪归正

　　qù xié guī zhèng

　　　　give up evil and return to good

何去何从

　　hé qù hé cóng

　　　　decide on what path to follow

【例句】Example

　　这是一个极好的避暑去处。

　　　　zhè shì yí gè jí hǎo de bì shǔ qù chù

　　　　　　This is a very nice place for summer.

rén

(human being; person; people)

丿 人

最古老的甲骨文里，"人"字有头，有手，还有脚（﹖），后来这字渐渐简化成只有两只脚的"人"。不过就算是这个样子，当我们一看见这字，依然觉得它像一个人。中国汉字就这样神奇，有时看形状就知道它的意义。

The earliest known pictographs of this very important character showed the figure of a person in profile — head, hands, and legs (﹖). This evolved stylistically towards the present form, two strokes that appear to show the legs in frontal view. The original pictographs may suggest an insight into man's evolution from the anthropoids—or even earlier forms of life—and this, in turn, suggests a link with prehistoric knowledge now all but lost to us.

【部首】 Radical　　人(亻)(person)

【同部首字】 Characters under the radical
　　仁(benevolence)，价(price)，他(he; him)

【词语】 Words and phrases

人格	réngé	personality
人类	rénlèi	humanity
人民	rénmín	people
人权	rénquán	human rights

人生	rénshēng	life
人性	rénxìng	human nature

人情世故

rén qíng shì gù

worldly wisdom

人言可畏

rén yán kě wèi

Gossip is a fearful thing.

人去楼空

rén qù lóu kōng

The chamber is empty with the dear person gone away.

人生几何

rén shēng jǐ hé

How long is a man's life?

人无远虑，必有近忧

rén wú yuǎn lǜ, bì yǒu jìn yōu

A person who has no anxious thoughts for the future will find trouble right at hand.

【例句】 Example

三人行必有吾师焉。(from Confucius)

sān rén xíng bì yǒu wǔ shī yān

Three people being together, there must be one who can be my teacher.

山

shān

(mountain)

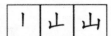

这个字早期是由三座并排的山组成（Ⅲ），合起来就成了一座大山。后来为了方便书写，每一座山都用一笔来表示，变成了现在的"山"字了。

The earlier form was clearly a pictographic representation of three peaks standing side by side (Ⅲ), creating the form and shape of a large mountain. Later, for the sake of convenience in writing, the peaks developed into single strokes.

【部首】Radical   山(mountain)

【同部首字】Characters under the radical
　　峰(peak)，岩(rock)，岸(coast)

【词语】 Words and phrases

山城	shānchéng	mountain city
山顶	shāndǐng	the summit of the mountain
山洞	shāndòng	cave
山冈	shāngǎng	low hill
山谷	shāngǔ	mountain valley
山岭	shānlǐng	mountain ridge
山区	shānqū	mountainous area

山盟海誓

    shān méng hǎi shì

      (make) a solemn pledge of love

山明水秀

    shān míng shuǐ xiù

      green hills and clear waters

        i.e., picturesque scenery

山南海北

    shān nán hǎi běi

      south of the mountains and north of the seas

        i.e., all over the land; far and wide

山外有山，天外有天

    shān wài yǒu shān, tiān wài yǒu tiān

      There are mountains beyond mountains, and heavens beyond heavens.

        i.e., There is always something or somebody better; one should be always modest.

山穷水尽疑无路，柳暗花明又一村

    shān qióng shuǐ jìn yí wú lù, liǔ àn huā míng yòu yì cūn

      When the mountains and rivers come to an end and one would think there is no path, the shady willows and bright blossoms bring him to another village.

【例句】Example

    中国和缅甸是山水相连的友好邻国。

      zhōng guó hé miǎn diàn shì shān shuǐ xiāng lián de yǒu hǎo líng guó

        China and Burma are friendly neighbours linked by mountains and rivers.

shàng

(above; upper)

丨	卜	上

"上" 字是由上下两条横线（二）组成，下面那条是地平线；上面那条是"在地平线之上"的意思，后来则变成为（⊥）。

The form of 上 on the oracle bones was represented by two horizontal lines(二); the one below indicates the "horizon" and the one above indicates "above the horizon". Later the form of the upper horizontal line was stylized a little (⊥), and the meaning of the character has also become clearer.

【部首】 Radical   —(horizontal line)

【同部首字】 Characters under the radical
　　无(without)，五(five)，不(no)

【词语】 Words and phrases

上班	shàngbān	go to work
上宾	shàngbīn	distinguished guest
上层	shàngcéng	upper strata; upper levels
上当	shàngdàng	be taken in; be fooled
上等	shàngděng	first-class; superior
上帝	shàngdì	God
上古	shànggǔ	ancient times

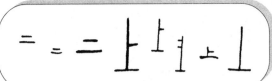

上级	shàngjí	higher authorities
上街	shàngjiē	go into the street
上课	shàngkè	attend class
上面	shàngmian	above; on the top of
上司	shàngsi	superior; boss

上行下效

shàng xíng xià xiào

What those above do, those below will follow.

i.e., People follow the examples of their superiors.

上达下情

shàng dá xià qíng

make the situation at the lower level known to the higher authorities

上刀山，下火海

shàng dāo shān, xià huǒ hǎi

climb a mountain of swords or plunge into a sea of flames

i.e., undergo the most severe trials

上梁不正下梁歪

shàng liáng bú zhèng xià liáng wāi

If the upper beams are not in the right position (straight), the lower ones are out of plumb (will go aslant).

i.e., When those above behave unworthily, those below will do the same.

上气不接下气

shàng qì bù jiē xià qì

i.e., be out (short) of breath

上天无路，入地无门

shàng tiān wú lù, rù dì wú mén

There is no road to the heaven and no door into the earth.

i.e., at the end of the hope

【例句】Example

时间到了，快上飞机吧!

shí jiān dào le, kuài shàng fēi jī ba

It's time to get on the plane!

少

shǎo

(less; few; little)

丿	丷	小	少

　　"少"的构成很有意思，在小（丷）字上再加一撇（丿）就变成"少"，就是指"数量不多"。

The character 少 is a combination of (丷) "small" and (丿) which indicates cutting something smaller. As it is smaller, it is of course less. Another saying is that the original form of the character was four dots which represented sand; later the third dot became longer, seeming to imply the location of the sand.

【部首】Radical　　　小(small)

【同部首字】Characters under the radical
　　劣(bad)，光(light)，尖(sharp)

【词语】Words and phrases

少不得	shǎo bù dé	cannot do without
少刻	shǎokè	after a little while
少量	shǎoliàng	a small amount
少陪	shǎopéi	if you'll excuse me
少数	shǎoshù	small number; minority
少数民族	shǎoshù mínzú	national minority
少许	shǎoxǔ	a little

少见多怪

    shǎo jiàn duō guài

       comment excitedly on a commonplace thing

          i.e., out of ignorance or inexperience

少说为妙

    shǎo shuō wéi miào

      The less said the better.

少智为福

    shǎo zhì wéi fú

      Ignorance is bliss.

少食多餐

    shǎo shí duō cān

      have more meals a day but less food at each

【例句】Example

    最近我很少见到他。

      zuì jìn wǒ hěn shǎo jiàn dào tā

        I have seen very little of him recently.

身

shēn

(body)

丿　亻　勹　勺　身　身　身

　　"身"就是指身体、身躯。这个字在甲骨文里表示"怀孕"，它画出一个肚子隆起的人，正用一只脚向前倾以平衡身体（图）。到了现在，人们仍然用"有了身子"来形容怀了孕的妇女。

This character originally meant "pregnant", and depicted a human figure with a prominent belly and one leg thrust forward for support and balance ( ). The modern form means the "human body".

【部首】Radical　　身(body)

【同部首字】Characters under the radical
　　躲(hide)，躯(body)，躺(lie)

【词语】Words and phrases

身边	shēnbiān	at (or by) one's side
身材	shēncái	figure
身长	shēncháng	height (of a person)
身价	shēnjià	social status
身躯	shēnqū	body; stature
身世	shēnshì	life experience
身手	shēnshǒu	skill

| 身体 | shēntǐ | body; health |
| 身心 | shēnxīn | body and mind |

身不由己
> shēn bù yóu jǐ
>> involuntarily

身经百战
> shēn jīng bǎi zhàn
>> have fought a hundred battles

身临其境
> shēn lín qí jìng
>> be personally on the scene

身体力行
> shēn tǐ lì xíng
>> earnestly practise what one advocates

身先士卒
> shēn xiān shì zú
>> lead one's men in a charge

【例句】 Example
> 这套衣服很合身。
>> zhè tào yī fú hěn hé shēn
>>> this suit fits (the body) perfectly

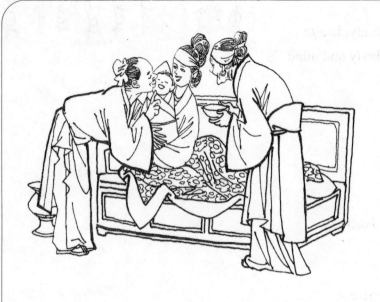

shēng

(grow)

丿 ㇒ 牛 生 生

"生"字最底下的一划代表地面，地面上长出了幼苗（ 业 ）。后来字形变了，才变成了如今的"生"字。这个字本来指草和树木的生长，后来又有"生存"和"活"的意思；还可以用来指未煮过的食物。

The original character 生 was a very vivid pictographic representation of a growing seedling (业):the horizontal stroke at the bottom of the character indicates the land; on the land a small seedling appears to have just broken through the soil, growing with vitality. Later the horizontal stroke turned into (土) "soil", and the seedling became like the shoot of a tree; finally the "tree" lost its shape and the character has become like the one we see today. The original meaning of 生 was precisely the growth of grass or a tree; later it was extended to mean "alive" or "living"; it was also borrowed to mean "raw".

【部首】 Radical 丿 (left-falling)

【同部首字】 Characters under the radical
升(rise)，千(thousand)，午(noon)

【词语】 Words and phrases

生词	shēngcí	new word
生产	shēngchǎn	produce
生存	shēngcún	live; exist

生动　　　shēngdòng　　lively
生活　　　shēnghuó　　life
生理　　　shēnglǐ　　　physiology
生日　　　shēngrì　　　birthday

生不逢时
　　shēng bù féng shí
　　　　be born at a wrong time
生老病死
　　shēng lǎo bìng sǐ
　　　　birth, age, illness and death
生灵涂炭
　　shēng líng tú tàn
　　　　plunge the people into misery and suffering
生龙活虎
　　shēng lóng huó hǔ
　　　　doughty as a dragon and lively as a tiger
　　　　　　i.e., full of vim and vigor
生米煮成熟饭
　　shēng mǐ zhǔ chéng shú fàn
　　　　The rice is cooked.
　　　　　　i.e., What's done can't be undone.
生死之交
　　shēng sǐ zhī jiāo
　　　　friendship between the two sharing each other's fate
生有涯而知无限
　　shēng yǒu yá ér zhī wú xiàn
　　　　Life is limited, but knowledge is limitless.
生于忧患，死于安乐
　　shēng yú yōu huàn, sǐ yú ān lè
　　　　Misery and affliction make a man diligent, and so he lives; peace
　　　　and happiness make a man lazy, and so he perishes.

【例句】 Example
　　我生在中国，长在中国。
　　　　wǒ shēng zài zhōng guó, zhǎng zài zhōng guó
　　　　　　I was born in China and grew up in China.

声

shēng

(sound)

| 一 | 十 | 士 | 芏 | 声 | 声 | 声 |

"声"（）由四部分组成：（ ）是倒转的钟，（ ）是持有敲钟棍的手，（ ）是耳朵，（ ）是口。它的意思相信也不难猜吧！当说话和音乐进入耳朵时，就变成了声音。

The upper left part of this character is in the shape of a inverted bell ( ); to the right is a hand holding a bell stick ( ) while in the middle is an ear ( ) and a mouth ( ). Therfore the whole picture indicates that words and music entering the ears is "sound".

【部首】 Radical　　士(soldier)

【同部首字】 Characters under the radical
　　吉(auspicious)，志(ambition)，喜(happy)

【词语】 Words and phrases

声波	shēngbō	sound wave
声调	shēngdiào	tone
声名	shēngmíng	reputation
声明	shēngmíng	state; declare
声势	shēngshì	impetus
声望	shēngwàng	popularity
声响	shēngxiǎng	sound; noise
声言	shēngyán	profess

| 声音 | shēngyīn | sound; voice |
| 声誉 | shēngyù | reputation; fame |

声东击西

    shēng dōng jī xī

        feint to the east but attack in the west

声泪俱下

    shēng lèi jù xià

        loud and bitter weeping

声名赫赫

    shēng míng hè hè

        to have awe-inspiring fame

声名狼籍

    shēng míng láng jí

        be notorious

声色俱厉

    shēng sè jù lì

        stern in voice and countenance

声势浩大

    shēng shì hào dà

        great in strength and impetus

【例句】Example

    我们听到远处有各种奇怪的声音。

        wǒ mén tīng dào yuǎn chù yǒu gè zhǒng qí guài de shēng yīn

        We heard strange sounds in the distance.

shuāng

(two; twin; both; dual)

ㄱ　ㄡ　刄　双

你看这个字形像不像一只右手（ㄟ）正捉着两只小鸟（𨿳）？既然与数量有关，所以就成了量词。世界上有很多东西都是成双成对的，好像我们的手、脚、耳朵、眼睛等。

The original form of the character 双 was a complex one, the upper part depicts two "birds" (𨿳) with their beaks turned to the left, sitting on a "right hand" (ㄟ). This combination indicates one hand catching two birds, which suggests the concept of "a pair".

【部首】 Radical　　　又(again)

【同部首字】 Characters under the radical
　　欢(happy)，受(accept)，对(correct)

【词语】 Words and phrases

双重	shuāngchóng	double
双方	shuāngfāng	both side
双幅	shuāngfú	double width
双关	shuāngguān	having a double meaning
双亲	shuāngqīn	father and mother
双手	shuāngshǒu	both hands
双数	shuāngshù	even numbers
双双	shuāngshuāng	in pairs

双喜　　　　shuāngxǐ　　　　double happiness

双双对对

　　shuāng shuāng duì duì

　　　　in pairs and couples

双宿双飞

　　shuāng sù shuāng fēi

　　　　always keep each other's company

双喜临门

　　shuāng xǐ lín mén

　　　　A double blessing has descended upon the house.

双管齐下

　　shuāng guǎn qí xià

　　　　paint a picture with two brushes at the same time

　　　　　　i.e., work along both lines

【例句】Example

　　这布是单幅还是双幅?

　　　　zhè bù shì dān fú hái shì shuāng fú

　　　　　　Is this cloth single or double width?

水

shuǐ

(water)

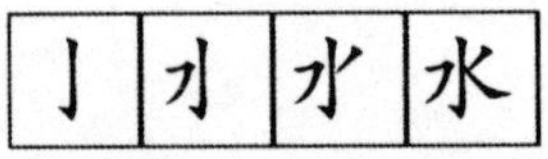

你说“水”字像不像一条河流（ ）？河流四周被很多水点围住（ ），一看便知道是水。用水作部首的字多数跟河流、水份、液体有关。水对人类来说极其重要，因为人体缺少了水便不能生存。

The original character 水 was formed by a stream in the middle ( ) with dots on both sides ( ) representing drops of water. In the inscriptions on oracle bones, the number of “drops” of water varied, but later it was fixed as two for each side. Gradually it developed to the form we see today. 水 as a radical is usually written as (氵). Chinese characters with this radical mostly have something to do with water.

【部首】Radical　　水(氵)(water)

【同部首字】Characters under the radical

河(river)，流(flow)，沙(sand)

【词语】Words and phrases

水兵	shuǐbīng	seaman
水彩	shuǐcǎi	watercolour
水产	shuǐchǎn	aquatic product
水池	shuǐchí	pool; pond
水电	shuǐdiàn	water and electricity

水管	shuǐguǎn	waterpipe
水果	shuǐguǒ	fruit
水晶	shuǐjīng	crystal
水力	shuǐlì	waterpower

水到渠成

shuǐ dào jú chéng

When water flows, a channel is formed.

i.e., When conditions are ripe, success will come.

水滴石穿

shuǐ dī shí chuān

Dripping water wears through rock.

i.e., constant effort brings success

水中捞月

shuǐ zhōng lāo yuè

fish for the moon in the water

i.e., make impractical or vain effort

水火不容

shuǐ huǒ bù róng

no intercourse between water and fire

水落石出

shuǐ luò shí chū

When the water subsides the rocks emerge.

i.e., The whole thing comes to light.

水涨船高

shuǐ zhǎng chuán gāo

When the river rises the boat goes up.

水有源，树有根

shuǐ yǒu yuán, shù yǒu gēn

Every river has its source and every tree has its roots.

i.e., Everything has its origin.

【例句】 Example

天气热，多喝点儿水。

tiān qì rè, duō hē diǎnr shuǐ

It's very hot, you should drink more water.

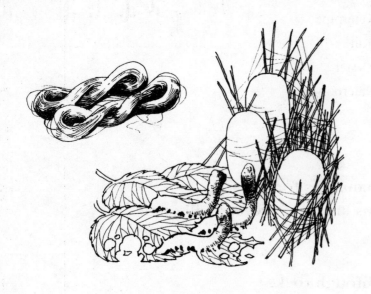

丝

sī

(silk)

∠	⅃	⅄	纟纟	丝

丝（絲）像两卷捆在一起的丝线，指的当然是蚕丝。因为丝线很细，所以人们会用"丝"来形容精致的东西，古代有些乐器也是用丝线制造的。

This was a pictogram of two reels of silk threads tied together (絲), meaning cocoon silk. Because silk thread is very fine and thin, 丝 was later used to describe things that were very delicate. Moreover, 丝 also meant string instruments in ancient China, and 竹 (zhú: bamboo) meant woodwind instruments.

【部首】 Radical —(horizontal line)

【同部首字】Characters under the radical
正(just)，亘(extend)，韭(leek)

【词语】 Words and phrases

丝绸	sīchóu	silk cloth
丝带	sīdài	silk ribbon
丝瓜	sīguā	towel gourd
丝光	sīguāng	the silky luster of mercerized cotton fabrics
丝毫	sīháo	the slightest amount or degree
丝绵	sīmián	silk floss
丝绒	sīróng	velvet

丝线	sīxiàn	silk thread
丝织品	sīzhīpǐn	silk fabrics
丝竹	sīzhú	traditional stringed and woodwind instruments; music

丝毫不差

    sī háo bú chà

        not err by a hair's breadth

丝毫不苟

    sī háo bù gǒu

        not in the least careless

丝丝入扣

    sī sī rù kòu

        done with flawless skill

丝竹管弦

    sī zhú guǎn xián

        music of string and flute

丝恩发怨

    sī ēn fà yuàn

        gratitude for the slightest favour received or grudge against the slightest wrong done

【例句】Example

    丝绸之路值得一游。

        sī chóu zhī lù zhí dé yì yóu

        It is worthwhile to take a trip to the Silk Road.

天

tiān

(sky; heaven)

一	二	天	天

这个字最初是一个没有头部的身体（夬），后来加上了头部（夬）变成"天"。"天"主宰宇宙万物，地位至高无上；因此以"一"、"大"组成的"天"，就说明了一切事物中最大的便是"天"。

(夬) represented the form of man, but it was only a body without the head. Then a "head" was added above the space of the body and it became (夬). So originally, 天 indicated "the head" of a man's body. At the beginning this "head" was as round as a ball, but later it gradually became flat, and finally it became a horizontal stroke like in the modern version. As the growing light of the sky brings in the dawn of the day, 天 also came to mean "day".

【部首】 Radical　　一(horizontal line)

【同部首字】 Characters under the radical
　　三(three)，上(above)，下(below)

【词语】 Words and phrases

天才	tiāncái	genius
天地	tiāndì	heaven and earth
天空	tiānkōng	the sky
天亮	tiānliàng	daybreak; dawn
天气	tiānqì	weather

天然	tiānrán	natural
天生	tiānshēng	born; inborn
天堂	tiāntáng	paradise

天长地久

    tiān cháng dì jiǔ

        as long as the heaven and the earth endure

天从人愿

    tiān cóng rén yuàn

        Heaven follows man's wish.

天马行空

    tiān mǎ xíng kōng

        a heavenly steed soaring across the skies

            i.e., a powerful and unconstrained style

天网恢恢，疏而不漏

    tiān wǎng huī huī, shū ér bú lòu

        The net of heaven has large meshes, but it lets nothing through.

            i.e., Justice has long arms.

天下本无事，庸人自扰之

    tiān xià běn wú shì, yōng rén zì rǎo zhī

        There is nothing wrong under heaven originally, the philistine worries about troubles of his own imagination.

天下乌鸦一般黑

    tiān xià wū yā yì bān hēi

        All crows under heaven are black.

天下无难事，只怕有心人

    tiān xià wú nán shì, zhǐ pà yǒu xīn rén

        All difficulties on the earth can be overcome if men but to give their minds to it.

            i.e., Where there is a will, there is a way.

【例句】 Example

    我在北京待了三天。

        wǒ zài běi jīng dāi le sān tiān

            I have stayed in Beijing for three days.

土

tǔ

(soil; earth)

一	十	土

这个字是指田地上的一堆土壤（ ）, 上面的部分表示土堆, 下面的一横表示土地。

土 is a pictograph which shows a pile of soil in a field ( ). The upper part represents the soil and the lower part represents the field.

【部首】Radical　　　土(earth)

【同部首字】Characters under the radical
　　基(base)，堆(pile)，域(territory)

【词语】Words and phrases

土产	tǔchǎn	local product
土地	tǔdì	land
土话	tǔhuà	local dialect
土皇帝	tǔhuángdì	local despot
土木	tǔmù	construction
土壤	tǔrǎng	soil
土人	tǔrén	native
土著	tǔzhù	original inhabitants

土崩瓦解

    tǔ bēng wǎ jiě

        fall apart

土豪劣绅

    tǔ háo liè shēn

        local tyrants and evil gentry

土生土长

    tǔ shēng tǔ zhǎng

        locally born and bred

土洋结合

    tǔ yáng jié hé

        combine indigenous and foreign methods

【例句】Example

    这儿的土壤很肥沃。

        zhèr de tǔ rǎng hěn féi wò

           The soil here is very fertile.

王

wáng

(king)

| 一 | 二 | 干 | 王 |

在 "人" 的上下都加上一笔，本来张开的双腿也合起来，变成一条直线，就构成了 "王" 字。人们常说三条横线分别代表天、地、人，要是能身体力行把人、天、地贯通起来，就是 "王"。

王 is formed by adding a horizontal stroke under the "person" (太) and another horizontal stroke above the "person" (天). As the two "legs" of the "person" close together, they become a vertical stroke. It is said that the three horizontal strokes represent the heaven, the earth, and the person. The person who could join the three together is the king.

【部首】Radical   王(king)

【同部首字】Characters under the radical
环(ring)，望(watch)，球(ball)

【词语】Words and phrases

王朝	wángcháo	imperial court; dynasty
王储	wángchǔ	crown prince
王法	wángfǎ	the law of the land
王宫	wánggōng	palace
王冠	wángguān	imperial crown; royal crown
王国	wángguó	kingdom

王侯	wánghóu	princes and marquises
王后	wánghòu	queen; queen consort
王室	wángshì	royal family
王位	wángwèi	throne
王子	wángzǐ	prince

王法无亲

wáng fǎ wú qīn

The law has no respecter of person.

王公贵族

wáng gōng guì zú

the nobility

王者以民为天

wáng zhě yǐ mín wéi tiān

A king's life depends upon the people.

王子犯法，与民同罪

wáng zǐ fàn fǎ, yǔ mín tóng zuì

If a prince violates the law, he must be punished like an ordinary person.

【例句】Example

中国有句谚语："成者为王，败者为寇。"

zhōng guó yǒu jù yàn yǔ: "chéng zhě wéi wáng, bài zhě wéi kòu"

This is a Chinese idiom saying:" The one who wins becomes a king and the one who loses becomes a bandit."

xī

(west)

一 厂 冋 丙 西 西

"西" 原本是一个雀巢（），后来在雀巢上面加上一条象征鸟的弧线变成（），合起来就像雀鸟在巢上栖息的样子。当太阳在西边落下，就是雀鸟回巢的时候了。

The original form of 西 was drawn as a bird's nest( ) in the oracle bones, but it developed into a more complicated form later with the addition of a curve above the nest ( ) representing a bird. This change makes the meaning of this character clearer: when the sun falls to the west, birds return to their nests; and that is the origin of the meaning of this character 西 "west".

【部首】Radical　　西(west)

【同部首字】Characters under the radical
　　要(want)，票(ticket)

【词语】Words and phrases

西餐	xīcān	Western style food
西方	xīfāng	the west
西风	xīfēng	west wind
西瓜	xīguā	watermelon
西南	xīnán	southwest
西欧	Xī Ōu	Western Europe

西天	xītiān	Western Paradise
西洋	Xīyáng	the Western world
西药	xīyào	Western medicine
西装	xīzhuāng	Western-style clothes

西方净土

xī fāng jìng tǔ

the heavenly paradise (of Buddhism)

i.e., the happy land in the west

西风残照

xī fēng cán zhào

a setting sun in the west wind

西风落叶

xī fēng luò yè

the west wind and fallen leaves

i.e., an autumn scene

西窗剪烛

xī chuāng jiǎn zhú

the happy reunion of friends chatting together late at night

【例句】 Example

香港是个东西文化交汇的城市。

xiāng gǎng shì gè dōng xī wén huà jiāo huì de chéng shì

Hong Kong is a city with a blending culture of East and West.

xí

(learn)

ㄋ	ㄋ	习

　　繁体的"习"字的上半部，是一个"羽"字，像小鸟的翅膀（羽）。而下半部原本是"日"字，后来变做"白"字。两部分合起来就是说鸟儿在太阳底下学飞。学习是需要重复练习的，所以后来"习"字又有了"习惯"的意思。

　　This is a very interesting character. The perceptive reader may have already noticed that the upper part of this non-simplified character is a (羽) which we have learned means "feathers" or "wings". The lower part of the character (☉) is what relates to learning. The two parts together means a bird trying to learn how to fly and thus derives the meaning of "learn".

【部首】 Radical 　　　　ㄋ (one)

【同部首字】 Characters under the radical
　　习 (tricky)

【词语】 Words and phrases

温习	wēnxí	review
习见	xíjiàn	(of things) commonly seen
习气	xíqì	bad habit
习俗	xísú	custom
习题	xítí	exercises (in school work)

习性　　　　xíxìng　　　　habits and characteristics

习与性成

xí yǔ xìng chéng

Habits become one's second nature.

习以为常

xí yǐ wéi cháng

be used to sth.

习非成是

xí fēi chéng shì

Accept what is wrong as right as one grows accustomed to it.

习焉不察

xí yān bù chá

too accustomed to something to call it in question

【例句】Example

小王在温习功课。

xiǎo wáng zài wēn xí gōng kè

Xiao Wang is reviewing his lessons.

喜

xǐ

(happy; joy)

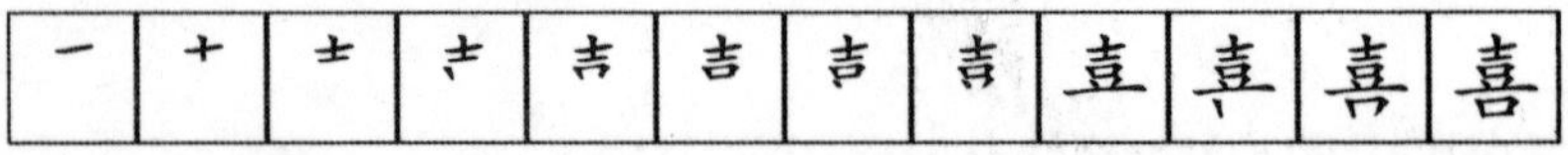

甲骨文里，“喜”（ ）的上部是鼓（ ），听到音乐使人有开心、快乐的感觉；下部是口（ ），人一开心就会开怀大笑，相信不难猜到它跟快乐、喜悦的情绪有关。此外，它还有喜欢、爱好和怀孕的含义。俗语说“有喜”，就是指“怀孕”。

In the oracle bones, this character was comprised of two parts: the upper part means “drum”( ) and the lower part means mouth ( ).“Drum” indicates “happy” or “joyful” feelings, and the “mouth” is a symbol of happy or joyful voices. So “happy”,“joyful” and “pleased” were the original meanings of this character. Later it was also extended to mean “to like” or “to be fond of ”, and also “pregnancy”.

【部首】Radical　　口(mouth)

【同部首字】Characters under the radical

后(back)，吐(vomit)，吵(noisy)

【词语】Words and phrases

喜爱	xǐ'ài	like; be fond of
喜冲冲	xǐchōngchōng	look exhilarated
喜欢	xǐhuān	like; be fond of
喜酒	xǐjiǔ	the wine drunk at a wedding
喜剧	xǐjù	comedy

喜庆	xǐqìng	joyous
喜事	xǐshì	happy event; wedding
喜讯	xǐxùn	happy news
喜悦	xǐyuè	happy; joyous

喜出望外
    xǐ chū wàng wài
       be overjoyed

喜怒不形于色
    xǐ nù bù xíng yú sè
       not show joy or anger on one's face

喜气洋洋
    xǐ qì yáng yáng
       full of joy

喜从天降
    xǐ cóng tiān jiàng
       unexpected good news comes from the sky

喜新厌旧
    xǐ xīn yàn jiù
       love the new and loathe the old

【例句】 Example
    郑先生喜欢在大海里游泳。
       zhèng xiān shēng xǐ huān zài dà hǎi lǐ yóu yǒng
         Mr. Zheng likes to swim in the sea.

xiān

(before; first)

ノ	⺊	十	生	歩	先

先字的字形，是（🦅）前面有脚步（业），表示已经走过的路，于是有"祖先"的意思。此外"先"也可解释为"前进"、"早于"或"在前"等含义。

A man facing left with a footprint above his head (𫞖), expressing the idea of "walking ahead". This is the original meaning of 先. Later the meaning was extended to include "before", "earlier" or "first".

【部首】Radical　　儿(son)

【同部首字】Characters under the radical
　　克(overcome)，兄(elder brother)

【词语】Words and phrases

先锋	xiānfēng	the vanguard
先进	xiānjìn	advanced
先例	xiānlì	precedent
先驱	xiānqū	pioneer; forerunner
先生	xiānsheng	mister; gentleman; sir
先天	xiāntiān	congenital; inborn

先入为主

    xiān rù wéi zhǔ

      First impressions are lasting impressions.

先声夺人

    xiān shēng duó rén

      forestall one's opponent by a show of strength

先睹为快

    xiān dǔ wéi kuài

      consider it a pleasure to be among the first to read (see) sth.

先礼后兵

    xiān lǐ hòu bīng

      trying courteous means before resorting to force

先天下之忧而忧，后天下之乐而乐

    xiān tiān xià zhī yōu ér yōu, hòu tiān xià zhī lè ér lè

      A leader should worry ahead of the people and enjoy the fruits after the people.

【例句】Example

    他先去北京，再去上海。

      tā xiān qù běi jīng, zài qù shàng hǎi

        He will go to Beijing first and then go to Shanghai.

小

xiǎo

(small)

| ⺌ | 小 | 小 |

 "小"由三条短直线（⺌）组成，通常指细小的物件。中间的直线（丨）指形状较小的物件，而两边的（丷）就是把小物件分开。如果我们将物件分开，它们的体积当然会比原来的小很多！

 The character 小 in the oracle bones was formed by three short verticals (⺌). The vertical in the middle depicts a small object and the other two on either side are the halves of a separated 八, which means "divide" as we know. When something is divided it naturally becomes "small".

【部首】 Radical 小\(small)

【同部首字】 Characters under the radical
 少(less, few)，尖(sharp)，尚(still)

【词语】 Words and phrases

小报	xiǎobào	tabloid
小吃	xiǎochī	snack; refreshment
小丑	xiǎochǒu	clown; buffoon
小贩	xiǎofàn	hawker; pedlar
小费	xiǎofèi	tip
小姐	xiǎojiě	Miss; young lady

小事	xiǎoshì	petty thing
小说	xiǎoshuō	novel; fiction
小算盘	xiǎosuànpán	selfish calculation
小心	xiǎoxīn	take care; be careful
小学	xiǎoxué	primary school

小恩小惠

    xiǎo ēn xiǎo huì

       petty favours

小巫见大巫

    xiǎo wū jiàn dà wū

       seem like a pigmy compared with the devil

小不忍则乱大谋

    xiǎo bù rěn zé luàn dà móu

       A little impatience spoils great plans.

小患不治成大灾

    xiǎo huàn bú zhì chéng dà zāi

       A small leak can sink a great ship.

【例句】Example

    我买了一份小礼物给我女儿。

       wǒ mǎi le yí fèn xiǎo lǐ wù gěi wǒ nǚ ér

         I bought a small gift for my daughter.

孝

xiào

(filial piety)

一	十	土	尹	芗	孝	孝

　　"孝"字的上半部分是一个长发的驼背老人（𦐇），下半部分是一个小孩（𭕪），画的是老人家把手放在小孩头上走路的情形。这个字说出了中国传统文化社会里，孝顺、服从和尽心奉养父母是儿女应尽的本分。

　　The original shape of 孝 is also very interesting. Look at the upper part of the character you will find an old man with hunchback and long hair (𦐇) and the lower part was a child (𭕪) as we already know. The old man has put his hand on the head of the child, and the child is supporting him while walking (孝). What the character means is exactly what it shows:"filial piety towards old people", which is one of the most important element in traditional Chinese culture.

【部首】 Radical　　　子(son)

【同部首字】 Characters under the radical
　　　孤(lonely)，孩(child)

【词语】 Words and phrases
带孝	dàixiào	in mourning
孝道	xiàodào	filial piety
孝敬	xiàojìng	give presents (to one's elders or superiors)
孝顺	xiàoshùn	show filial obedience

孝子	xiàozǐ	dutiful son

孝子贤孙

xiào zǐ xián sūn

dutiful sons and grandsons

i.e., worthy progeny

【例句】 Example

中国人很重视孝道。

zhōng guó rén hěn zhòng shì xiào dào

Chinese emphasize a lot on filial piety.

xīn

(heart; feeling; center)

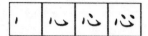

　　最初的"心"字，画出了心脏的形状（♡）。有两心房和两心室。后来，这字又指"思想"或"感情"。古人认为，心脏的位置是在胸部中央，于是它便有了"中间"、"核心"的含义。

　　This character is a primitive anatomical representation of a heart. The original meaning of 心 is "the heart"; it was also extended to mean "mind" or "feelings". As the ancients thought that the heart was in the middle of the chest, it has also been extended to mean "center" or "core".

【部首】Radical　　　心(heart)

【同部首字】Characters under the radical
　　忠(loyal)，忘(forget)，念(read; thinking)

【词语】Words and phrases

心爱	xīn'ài	love; treasure
心地	xīndì	a person's character; moral nature
心肝	xīngān	conscience; darling
心理	xīnlǐ	psychology
心情	xīnqíng	mood
心事	xīnshì	a load on one's mind; worry

| 心思 | xīnsī | thought; idea |
| 心愿 | xīnyuàn | cherished desire; wish |

心不在焉

xīn bú zài yān

absent-minded

心高气傲

xīn gāo qì ào

proud and arrogant

心狠手辣

xīn hěn shǒu là

hard-hearted and cruel

心灰意懒

xīn huī yì lǎn

One's heart sinks.

心旷神怡

xīn kuàng shén yí

free of mind, happy of heart

心猿意马

xīn yuán yì mǎ

One's heart is agile as an ape and one's thoughts swift as a horse.

心照不宣

xīn zhào bù xuān

understand each other without anything being spelt (out)

心有余而力不足

xīn yǒu yú ér lì bù zú

one's ability falls short of one's wish

心像平原走马，易放难收

xīn xiàng píng yuán zǒu mǎ, yì fàng nán shōu

The mind is like a horse on the plain, easy to let go but difficult to stop.

【例句】 Example

他人在这儿，心却不在。

tā rén zài zhèr, xīn què bú zài

He himself is here, but his thoughts are not.

信

xìn

(confidence; believe; letter;
correspondence)

丿 亻 亻 亻 仁 信 信 信 信

　　"信" 字是由 "人" 和 "言" 组成的字，表示人说的话应该是真实的，所以 "信" 的原意就是指 "实话"、"诚实"。后来这个字又多了不少的意义，比方 "信心"、"相信" 等等。

　　The character 信 is an associative compound comprised of 人 (rén: person) on the left and 言 (yán: speech/word) on the right, signifying that the words of a person should be true. So the original meaning of this character was "words being true and honest"; it has also been extended to mean "confidence","to believe", and "letter", etc.

【部首】 Radical　　人 (亻)(person)

【同部首字】 Characters under the radical
　　你(you)，佳(good)，伯(uncle)

【词语】 Words and phrases
信贷	xìndài	credit
信封	xìnfēng	envelope
信奉	xìnfèng	believe in
信服	xìnfú	completely accept
信号	xìnhào	signal
信件	xìnjiàn	mail, letters
信念	xìnniàn	belief; faith

信任	xìnrèn	trust
信息	xìnxī	information
信箱	xìnxiāng	letter box
信心	xìnxīn	confidence

信誓旦旦

xìn shì dàn dàn

pledge in all sincerity and seriousness

信赏必罚

xìn shǎng bì fá

due rewards and punishments will be meted out without fail

信口雌黄

xìn kǒu cí huáng

wag one's tongue too freely

i.e., make irresponsible remarks

信口开河

xìn kǒu kāi hé

wag one's tongue too freely

i.e., talk nonsense

信守诺言

xìn shǒu nuò yán

keep one's promise

【例句】 Example

他不是一个可以信赖的人。

tā bú shì yí gè kě yǐ xìn lài de rén

He's not the sort of man to be trusted.

休

xiū

(rest)

丿 亻 亻 什 休 休

"休"是由人（亻）和木（木）组成，指一个人倚在树旁休息，所以有"休止"和"歇息"的意思。后来这字又有了"不要"的意思。

休 is a combination of (亻) and (木), picturing a person resting against a tree, signifying "rest" 休息. From this original meaning, it was extended to mean "stop", as in 争论不休 (zhēng lùn bù xiū:"argue without stop"). From "stop", it was borrowed to mean "don't", as in 休要胡说 (xiū yào hú shuō:"don't talk nonsense").

【部首】Radical   亻 (person)

【同部首字】Characters under the radical
    仅(only)，他(he; him)，伤(wound)

【词语】Words and phrases

休假	xiūjià	have holiday
休息	xiūxi	have a rest; rest
休闲	xiūxián	casual
休学	xiūxué	suspend one's schooling without losing one's status as a student
休养	xiūyǎng	recuperate
休战	xiūzhàn	cease-fire

休养生息

    xiū yǎng shēng xī

       rest and build up strength

休弃前嫌

    xiū qì qián xián

       repudiate a previous grievance

休戚相关

    xiū qì xiāng guān

       mutually concerned in case of good or bad turn

争论不休

    zhēng lùn bù xiū

       argue ceaselessly

休要自夸

    xiū yào zì kuā

       Don't talk big.

【例句】Example

    今天我休息。

       jīn tiān wǒ xiū xī

         Today I'm off.

xuè

(blood)

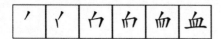

古代的"血"字，是在器皿上加上一划，表示器皿里盛载着血液，指用作祭祀拜神仪式的牲畜的血（血）。

The character 血 is represented by adding a horizontal stroke (●) on a vessel (血) indicating what the vessel holds is blood. The original meaning of 血 was the blood used for sacrificial rites.

【部首】Radical   血(blood)

【同部首字】Characters under the radical
    衅(dispute)

【词语】Words and phrases

血管	xuèguǎn	blood vessel
血汗	xuèhàn	blood and sweat
血肉	xuèròu	flesh and blood
血色	xuèsè	redness of the skin
血统	xuètǒng	blood relationship
血型	xuèxíng	blood group; blood type
血压	xuèyā	blood pressure
血液	xuèyè	blood

血缘　　　　　xuèyuán　　　　ties of blood

血口喷人

xuè kǒu pēn rén

cast malicious words to injure sb.

血脉相通

xuè mài xiāng tōng

be of one blood

血气方刚

xuè qì fāng gāng

full of sap

血肉相连

xuè ròu xiāng lián

be related by flesh and blood

血肉之躯

xuè ròu zhī qū

mortal flesh and blood

血浓于水

xuè nóng yú shuǐ

Blood is thicker than water.

【例句】Example

他受伤后流了很多血。

tā shòu shāng hòu liú le hěn duō xuè (xiě)

He has lost a lot of blood since he was injured.

炎

yán

(scorching)

、	丶	丷	火	火	炎	步	炎

　　一看这个字（炎）便知道是和"火"有关，而且火还烧得很旺呢，所以就指"烈火"，同时它也有"燃烧"的意思。

　　Two fires combined together, one atop the other, like flames licking the sky (炎), represents the idea of "a roaring fire." This is the original meaning of 炎. Then it was extended to mean "burn"; from "burn" it was also extended to mean "burning hot", as in 赤日炎炎 (chìrì yányán:"the scorching sun").

【部首】Radical　　火(fire)

【同部首字】Characters under the radical
　　炒(fry)，煤(coal)，烧(burn)

【词语】Words and phrases
炎热	yánrè	scorching; blazing
炎日	yánrì	scorching sun
炎夏	yánxià	hot summer
炎炎	yányán	scorching; blazing

炎黄子孙

　　yán huáng zǐ sūn

　　　　descendants of the Chinese nation

炎凉世态

　　yán liáng shì tài

　　　　the aspect of worldly affairs

炎附寒弃

　　yán fù hán qì

　　　　cleave to influential and wealthy persons and discard poor and mean
　　　　ones

赤日炎炎

　　chì rì yán yán

　　　　the blazing sun

【例句】Example

　　天气炎热，小心中暑。

　　　　tiān qì yán rè, xiǎo xīn zhòng shǔ

　　　　　　The weather is scorching. Be careful not to get sunstroke.

yán

(speech; word; to say)

以前的"言"字，底部画了一根舌头（舌），舌头之上有一条线，是指那舌头发出来的声音。如今，"言"字常用作部首，不少与说话、语言有关的字，都会用到它。

Originally the bottom part of the character was a drawing of a tongue (舌), and the vertical line above it represented the speech produced by the tongue. 言 can also be a radical. The characters using this radical have something to do with speech, language or morality.

【部首】Radical   言(讠)(speech)

【同部首字】Characters under the radical
    词(word)，讲(speak)，说(say)

【词语】 Words and phrases

言词	yáncí	one's words
言和	yánhé	make peace
言论	yánlùn	opinion on public affairs
言谈	yántán	the way one speaks or what he says
言行	yánxíng	words and deeds
言语	yányǔ	spoken language

言传身教

    yán chuán shēn jiào

      teach by words and lead by example

        i.e., to practise what you preach

言出必行

    yán shū bì xíng

      suit the action to the word

言为心声

    yán wéi xīn shēng

      Words are the voice of the mind.

言外之意

    yán wài zhī yì

      what one actually meant

言必信，行必果

    yán bì xìn, xíng bì guǒ

      always be true in word and resolute in deed

【例句】Example

    如果你老是食言，就没有人会再相信你。

    rú guǒ nǐ lǎo shì shí yán, jiù méi yǒu rén huì zài xiāng xìn nǐ

      If you always break your promises, no one will trust you any more.

羊

yáng

(sheep)

丶	丷	丷	丷	兰	羊

这是羊的正面轮廓（Ꮗ），两只角加上一个三角形的嘴就成了"羊"。后来三角形演变成一条直线和三条横线，加上头上的两只角就成为现在的"羊"字。羊在古时多用作祭祀，所以它便是"吉祥"的象征。

(Ꮗ) pictures the frontal view of a sheep: two horns and a triangle towards the bottom representing the mouth. Later the triangle was divided into one vertical stroke and three horizontal strokes; and this is how we write the character today.

【部首】Radical　　羊(sheep)

【同部首字】Characters under the radical
群(crowd)，美(pretty)，盖(cover)

【词语】Words and phrases

羊羔	yánggāo	lamb
羊倌	yángguān	shepherd
羊毫	yángháo	writing brush made of goat's hair
羊圈	yángjuàn	sheepfold
羊毛	yángmáo	sheep's wool
羊皮	yángpí	sheepskin
羊绒	yángróng	cashmere

羊肉　　　　　　yángròu　　　　mutton

羊落虎口

　　yáng luò hǔ kǒu

　　　a sheep fallen into the tiger's mouth

羊入狼群

　　yáng rù láng qún

　　　a sheep entering a pack of wolves

羊群里头出骆驼

　　yáng qún lǐ tóu chū luò tuó

　　　stand out like a camel in a flock of sheep

羊肉不曾吃，空惹一身膻

　　yáng ròu bù céng chī, kōng rě yì shēn shān

　　　not having eaten the mutton but instead invited a strong smell all of the body

　　　　i.e., not having got any advantage but invited trouble

羊毛出在羊身上

　　yáng máo chū zài yáng shēn shàng

　　　After all, the wool still comes from the sheep's back.

　　　　i.e., In the long turn, whatever you are given, you pay for.

【例句】Example

　　北京的涮羊肉很出名。

　　　běi jīng de shuàn yáng ròu hěn chū míng

　　　　The instant-boiled mutton in Beijing is very well-known.

养

yǎng

(raise)

| 、 | ⺀ | ⺞ | ⺞ | 兰 | 羊 | 关 | 养 | 养 |

　　"养"（🐑）的左边是一只羊（🐑），右边是拿着鞭子的手（✍），一看便猜到是放羊。

The original form of (🐑) was a combination of (🐑) "sheep" on the left and a right hand (✍) with a vertical strokes on the right. This suggests putting a sheep to pasture with a hand holding a whip.

【部首】 Radical　　羊(sheep)

【同部首字】 Characters under the radical
　　羞(shy)，差(bad)，姜(ginger)

【词语】 Words and phrases

养病	yǎngbìng	recuperate
养分	yǎngfèn	nutrient
养活	yǎnghuo	support; feed
养料	yǎngliào	nutriment
养神	yǎngshén	rest and attain mental tranquility
养生	yǎngshēng	preserve one's health
养育	yǎngyù	bring up
养鱼池	yǎngyúchí	fishpond

养而不教

 yǎng ér bú jiào

  bear the children without educating them

养儿防老

 yǎng ér fáng lǎo

  raise children to provide against old age

养虎为患

 yǎng hǔ wéi huàn

  nourish a tiger to source of trouble in future

养精蓄锐

 yǎng jīng xù ruì

  conserve one's strength and store up energy

养老送终

 yǎng lǎo sòng zhōng

  provide for the aged parent(s) and amend upon their funeral(s)

养性修身

 yǎng xìng xiū shēn

  promote conduct and practise ethics

养尊处优

 yǎng zūn chǔ yōu

  enjoy in a high position and live in ease and comfort

养兵千日，用兵一时

 yǎng bīng qiān rì, yòng bīng yì shí

  Troops are kept a thousand days to be used on one day.

【例句】Example

 我们要感激父母的养育之恩。

  wǒ mén yào gǎn jī fù mǔ de yǎng yù zhī ēn

   We must gratitude to our parents for their love and care for us.

夜

yè

(night)

| 丶 | 亠 | 广 | 亣 | 疒 | 疔 | 夜 | 夜 |

"夜"字画得像一个站直身的人（），加在人右臂下的一点（丿），是指"腋窝"；至于左臂下的那个"月"字（⺝），代表月亮慢慢升到腋窝那个位置，即黑夜已降临大地，也是休息的时候了。

This character originated from the pictograph (), which is a drawing of a person standing straight. By adding a dot (丿) under the right arm of the person, it means underarm. Then by putting a (⺝) 月yuè " the moon" under the left arm of the person, it means the moon has risen to the height of a person's underarm. This indicates that nighttime has arrived. Therefore () means "night". After thousands of years, () has changed to 夜 , but the meaning still remains.

【部首】Radical　　亠(above)

【同部首字】Characters under the radical
变(change)，交(cross)，享(enjoy)

【词语】Words and phrases

夜半	yèbàn	midnight
夜车	yèchē	night train
夜航	yèháng	night flight or navigation
夜间	yèjiān	at night

夜幕	yèmù	curtain of night
夜色	yèsè	the dim light of night
夜宵	yèxiāo	food taken late at night
夜校	yèxiào	evening school
夜总会	yèzǒnghuì	night club

夜以继日

yè yǐ jì rì

day and night

夜不闭户

yè bú bì hù

doors were not closed at night

夜阑人静

yè lán rén jìng

in the still of night

夜郎自大

yè láng zì dà

as cheekily as Yelang (chief), who thinks himself the equal of the Son of Heaven

夜长梦多

yè cháng mèng duō

A long night gives rise to many dreams.

i.e., Heaven knows what may happen all this long while.

夜蛾赴火

yè é fù huǒ

a moth flying into the fire

i.e., seek one's own doom

【例句】 Example

上海的夜景非常迷人。

shàng hǎi de yè jǐng fēi cháng mí rén

The night scene of Shanghai is very charming.

yī

(clothes)

丶	亠	广	才	衣	衣

中国古时的衬衣就是这个样子（），（人）是衣领和衣袖；（也）是衣襟，不过现今的"衣"字早已失去了古时衬衣的特征。最初的"衣"字是指"衬衣"，后来才扩大至所有的衣服。

The shape of this character resembles an ancient Chinese-style shirt (衣). The (人) portion looks like the collar and two sleeves, and the (也) part of the character represents the part of the shirt which flaps over from left to right. Unfortunately, the 衣 nowadays has lost most of its interesting resemblance to the Chinese-style shirt. As the pictogram suggests, the character 衣 originally meant "shirt", but later generalizations extended its meaning to include clothes of all kinds.

【部首】 Radical　　衣(clothes)

【同部首字】 Characters under the radical
　　裂(crack)，裔(descendants)，哀(sorrow)

【词语】 Words and phrases

衣橱	yīchú	wardrobe
衣服	yīfu	clothing; clothes
衣冠	yīguān	hat and clothes
衣架	yījià	coat hanger

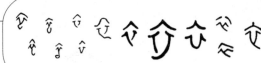

衣料	yīliào	material for clothing
衣物	yīwù	clothing and other articles of daily use
衣箱	yīxiāng	suitcase
衣着	yīzhuó	clothing, headgear and footwear

衣冠楚楚

yī guān chǔ chǔ

be dressed like a gentleman

衣冠禽兽

yī guān qín shòu

a beast in human clothing

i.e., a well dressed man of beastly temper

衣食住行

yī. shí zhù xíng

clothing, food, shelter and transportation

i.e., basic necessities of life

衣不如新，人不如故

yī bù rú xīn, rén bù rú gù

New clothes are best, and so are old friends

衣食足，然后知荣辱

yī shí zú, rán hòu zhī róng rǔ

Well fed, well bred.

衣沾不足惜，但使愿无违

yī zhān bù zú xī, dàn shǐ yuàn wú wéi

If I could follow my wish it would not matter if my clothes get soaked.

慈母手中线，游子身上衣

cí mǔ shǒu zhōng xiàn, yóu zǐ shēn shàng yī

The sewing at the mother's hands has become the coat on the wandering son's back.

【例句】 Example

中国有句古话：衣食足，然后知荣辱。

zhōng guó yǒu jù gǔ huà: yī shí zú, rán hòu zhī róng rǔ

There is an old saying in Chinese: Well fed, well bred.

友

yǒu

(friend; friendship)

| 一 | 广 | 方 | 友 |

　"友"即友爱，甲骨文里是两只手紧扣在一起，手牵手（州），用来表示互相合作，亦有交朋友的意思。后来为了方便书写，字形就由左右排列变成上下排列，变成了现在这个样子。

"Two right hands" close together (州) in the inscriptions on oracle bones gives us the sense of two people with each other's right hands clasping to show their friendship; the persons performing this action are, of course "friends". So "friend" is precisely what this character originally meant. Later, for the convenience of writing, the form was changed to have one hand above the other, and that is the modern version we see today.

【部首】Radical　　又(again)

【同部首字】Characters under the radical
　　反(against)，支(support)，受(accept)

【词语】Words and phrases

友爱	yǒu'ài	friendly
友邦	yǒubāng	friendly nation
友好	yǒuhǎo	friendly
友情	yǒuqíng	friendly sentiment
友人	yǒurén	friend

友谊   yǒuyì   friendship

良师益友

     liáng shī yì yǒu

         good teacher and helpful friend

狐朋狗友

     hú péng gǒu yǒu

         bad friends

酒肉朋友

     jiǔ ròu péng yǒu

         wine and meat friends

             i.e., friends in prosperity

友爱之谊

     yǒu ài zhī yì

         the friendliness of brothers

友好条约

     yǒu hǎo tiáo yuē

         treaty of friendship

【例句】 Example

     你真是我的良师益友。

         nǐ zhēn shì wǒ de liáng shī yì yǒu

             You are really my good teacher and helpful friend.

yǒu

(possess; have)

一 ナ 才 冇 冇 有

"有"字是在（◿）之下有一个（ᗞ），看上去像手拿着肉的样子。古时人们生活艰苦，有肉吃是很了不起的事，犹如拥有了全世界！所以衍生出"拥有"、"具有"的意思，"有"的反义词是"无"。

The ancient form of this character used the form (◿) on top of (ᗞ) which itself was a form of the character 肉 (ròu: meat). As a whole, it depicts a right hand holding a piece of meat. To the ancients, possessing meat was felt akin to owning the entire world, therefore a right hand holding onto a piece of meat meant "have" or "possess". Gradually this character came to be used as an antonym of " 无 " (nothing; not possessing)

【部首】 Radical   月(meat)

【同部首字】 Characters under the radical
    服(clothes)，胖(fat)，朝(toward)

【词语】 Words and phrases

有功	yǒugōng	have rendered great service
有鬼	yǒuguǐ	there is something fishy
有害	yǒuhài	harmful
有理	yǒulǐ	reasonable
有利	yǒulì	advantageous

有趣	yǒuqù	interesting; amusing
有限	yǒuxiàn	limited
有效	yǒuxiào	efficacious

有口皆碑

yǒu kǒu jiē bēi

win universal praise

有利可图

yǒu lì kě tú

have good prospects for gain

有备无患

yǒu bèi wú huàn

Where there is precaution, there is no danger.

有隙可乘

yǒu xī kě chéng

There is a crack to squeeze through.

有奶便是娘

yǒu nǎi biàn shì niáng

Whoever suckles me is my mother.

有眼不识泰山

yǒu yǎn bù shí tài shān

have eyes but fail to see Taishan Mountain

有则改之，无则加勉

yǒu zé gǎi zhī, wú zé jiā miǎn

correct mistakes if you have made any and guard against them if you have not

有志者事竟成

yǒu zhì zhě shì jìng chéng

Where there is a will there is a way.

【例句】 Example

我有一本汉英词典。

wó yǒu yì běn hàn yīng cí diǎn

I have a Chinese-English Dictionary.

鱼

yú

(fish)

丿 ⺈ ⺈ 鱼 鱼 鱼 鱼 鱼

象形字里是一条直立的鱼（）：头向上，尾向下。后来鱼身的图案被拉直变为笔画，而鱼尾则由一横代替。

This character depicts the abdomen of a fish (), with the head upwards and the tail downwards. Later developments had the body all straightened into strokes, and the tail became four dots. The simplified version of the character 鱼 even changed the four dots to a horizontal line.

【部首】Radical   鱼(fish)

【同部首字】Characters under the radical
鲁(stupid)，鲨(shark)，鲜(delicious)

【词语】Words and phrases

鱼翅	yúchì	shark's fin
鱼刺	yúcì	fishbone
鱼竿	yúgān	fishing rod
鱼肝油	yúgānyóu	cod-liver oil
鱼钩	yúgōu	fishhook
鱼鳞	yúlín	fish scale
鱼群	yúqún	shoal of fish

| 鱼子 | yúzǐ | roe |
| 鱼子酱 | yúzǐjiàng | caviare |

鱼龙混杂

yú lóng hùn zá

Dragons and fishes jumbled together.

i.e., Good and bad people mixed up.

鱼米之乡

yú mǐ zhī xiāng

a land of fish and rice

i.e., a land of plenty

鱼目混珠

yú mù hùn zhū

pass off fish eyes as pearls

i.e., pass off the sham as the genuine

鱼水情深

yú shuǐ qíng shēn

be closed as fish and water

如鱼得水

rú yú dé shuǐ

feel just like fish in water

【例句】 Example

中国的江南是鱼米之乡。

zhōng guó de jiāng nán shì yú mǐ zhī xiāng

The south of the Yangtze River is a land of plenty.

yǔ

(rain)

一　厂　冇　币　雨　雨　雨　雨

天空洒下来的雨，就是这个样子（🖼）的吧！甲骨文里"雨"字的那条横线代表云，下面六条较短的线是雨滴，后来再在雨水上面加多一横代表天，水从云中落下就是"雨"了。

The original pictograph for (🖼) showed rain pouring down from clouds at a high altitude. As inscribed on the oracle bones, the horizontal stroke indicates the clouds, and the six short lines hanging down indicate the raindrops. Later, another horizontal stroke was added above, most probably to indicate the "sky".

【部首】 Radical　　雨(rain)

【同部首字】 Characters under the radical
雪(snow)，霞(rosy clouds)，零(zero)

【词语】 Words and phrases

雨点	yǔdiǎn	raindrop
雨季	yǔjì	rainy season
雨具	yǔjù	rain gear
雨量	yǔliàng	rainfall
雨伞	yǔsǎn	umbrella
雨衣	yǔyī	raincoat

雨过天晴

    yǔ guò tiān qíng

        the sun shines after the rain

雨后春笋

    yǔ hòu chūn sǔn

        bamboo shoots after a spring rain

大雨倾盆

    dà yǔ qīng pén

        The rain is pelting down.

春风化雨

    chūn fēng huà yǔ

        the life-giving spring breeze and rain

           i.e., the salutary influence of education

【例句】 Example

    外面在下雨，出去别忘了带伞。

      wài miàn zài xià yǔ, chū qù bié wàng le dài sǎn

        It's raining outside. Don't forget to take the umbrella when you

        go out.

玉

yù

(jade)

一	二	干	王	玉

古人视玉器为珍宝，他们会用一条绳把三块玉系在一起，好好收藏。漂亮的玉器可以给人温暖、柔软和闪亮的感觉，所以它被用来形容一些漂亮的人和事物，像"玉颜"、"玉女"等。

In the oracle bones, this character is represented by a string tying three pieces of jade together. Ancient Chinese considered jade to be a treasure, so they used strings to tie pieces of them together. Because jade is a warm, soft and shiny gem stone, ancient people used the word to compliment beautiful and prestigious things, e.g. 玉颜(yù yán:" beautiful face of a woman"), 玉女(yù nǚ:"golden girl"), 玉成其事(yù chéng qí shì:"to finish a task beautifully").

【部首】 Radical   王(king)

【同部首字】 Characters under the radical
玩(play)，球(ball)，珍(precious)

【词语】 Words and phrases

玉成	yùchéng	kindly help make a success of something
玉带	yùdài	jade belt
玉雕	yùdiāo	jade carving
玉米	yùmǐ	maize

玉器	yùqì	jade article
玉色	yùsè	jade green
玉石	yùshí	jade

玉洁冰清

yù jié bīng qīng

as pure as jade and as clear as ice

玉石不分

yù shí bù fēn

make no distinction between jade and stone

玉液琼浆

yù yè qióng jiāng

top-quality wine

玉不琢，不成器

yù bù zhuó, bù chéng qì

If jade is not polished, it can not be made into anything.

i.e., spare the rod and spoil the child

【例句】 Example

这是一件玉石饰物。

zhè shì yí jiàn yù shí shì wù

This is a jade ornament.

月

yuè

(moon; month)

丿 | 几 | 月 | 月

　　平时我们看到的月亮多数是弯月，所以"月"字最初像一轮新月（☽）高挂在天空。后来人们在这个字中间加进一笔（☽），可能这一笔就是神话中的月桂树了。

　　As the moon spends more time in its waxing and waning stages than it does being full, the original pictograph 月 pictured a new moon hanging in the sky (☽). Later a vertical stroke was added inside the moon (☽) which was considered to indicate the bay tree as man imagined.

【部首】Radical　　　月(moon)

【同部首字】Characters under the radical
　　有(possess)，朋(friend)，肩(shoulder)

【词语】Words and phrases

月份	yuèfèn	month
月光	yuèguāng	moonlight
月刊	yuèkān	monthly magazine
月历	yuèlì	monthly calendar
月亮	yuèliang	the moon
月票	yuèpiào	monthly ticket
月台	yuètái	railway platform

月夜　　　yuèyè　　　moonlit night

月白风清
　　yuè bái fēng qīng
　　　　The moon is bright, the wind is soft.

月里嫦娥
　　yuè lǐ cháng é
　　　　legendary fairy of the moon

月下花前
　　yuè xià huā qián
　　　　under the moonlight and in front of the flowers
　　　　　　i.e., the place for lovers

月下老人
　　yuè xià lǎo rén
　　　　the old man under the moon
　　　　　　i.e., the God who unites persons in marriage

【例句】Example
　　一年有十二个月。
　　　　yì nián yǒu shí èr gè yuè
　　　　　　There are twelve months in a year.

云

yún

(cloud)

| 一 | 二 | 云 | 云 |

　　从它的字形可看到浮在空气中的云朵（⌒），十分有趣。上面两划（二）代表"云在空气之中形成"。

The original character for 云 pictured a floating cloud curling up into the air(⌒). The two short strokes on the upper part (二) form the ancient version of 上 "shàng", which represents the sky where the clouds are formed. Later, a 雨 was added on the top of 云 to imply the relationship between "clouds" and "rain". It was simplified again to its present form.

【部首】Radical　　二(two)

【同部首字】Characters under the radical
　　开(open)，元(first)，亏(lose)

【词语】Words and phrases

云彩	yúncǎi	cloud
云层	yúncéng	cloud layer
云海	yúnhǎi	a sea of cloud
云集	yúnjí	come together in crowds
云雀	yúnquè	skylark
云雾	yúnwù	cloud and mist

云霄	yúnxiāo	the skies
云霞	yúnxiá	rosy clouds
云烟	yúnyān	cloud and mist

云消雾散

yún xiāo wù sàn

The clouds melt and the mists disperse.

i.e., vanish in the air

过眼云烟

guò yǎn yún yān

as transient as a fleeting cloud

云出无心

yún chū wú xīn

The cloud arises without design.

云开见日

yún kāi jiàn rì

dispel the clouds and see the sun

【例句】Example

飞机在云层的上面飞行。

fēi jī zài yún céng de shàng miàn fēi xíng

The plane is flying above the clouds.

知

zhī

(know; be aware of; knowledge)

丶 乙 二 午 矢 知 知 知

这字由箭（矢）和口（口）组成，意思指很快便从别人的口中知道某些事情。

This character is a combination of (矢) "arrow" and (口) "mouth", implying that what one knows well can be spoken very quickly (like an arrow).

【部首】Radical   矢(arrow)

【同部首字】Characters under the radical
    矮(short)，短(short)

【词语】Words and phrases

知道	zhīdào	know
知己	zhījǐ	intimate friend
知觉	zhījué	consciousness; intuition
知名	zhīmíng	well-known; famous
知识	zhīshi	knowledge
知音	zhīyīn	a friend keenly appreciative of one's talents
知足	zhīzú	be content with one's lot

知己知彼

    zhī jǐ zhī bǐ

        know yourself as well as the enemy

            i.e., know both sides

知耻近乎勇

    zhī chǐ jìn hū yǒng

        Feeling shame is close to bravery.

知法犯法

    zhī fǎ fàn fǎ

        deliberately flout the law

            i.e., to know the law and violate it

知易行难

    zhī yì xíng nán

        To know is easy, to do is difficult.

知其不可为而为之

    zhī qí bù kě wéi ér wéi zhī

        to do something even while knowing it is impossible to succeed

知其然，不知其所以然

    zhī qí rán, bù zhī qí suó yǐ rán

        to know it is so, but not why it is so

知人者智，自知者明

    zhī rén zhě zhì, zì zhī zhě míng

        He who knows others is learned and he who knows himself is wise.

【例句】Example

    你要知道，如果你想成功，就得更努力。

        nǐ yào zhī dào, rú guǒ nǐ xiǎng chéng gōng, jiù děi gèng nǔ lì

            You'll have to try harder, you know, if you want to succeed.

止

zhǐ

(stop)

| 丨 | 卜 | 止 | 止 |

甲骨文的"止"字像一只脚（ᛂ），当这只脚不再向前走的时候，就会停下来。这个字的意义应该很清楚吧？

From the oracle bones, we can see that (ᛂ) characterizes the representation of a foot with the toes towards the left, and the heel to the right, so the original meaning of 止 is for "foot". When the feet don't move then they "stop"; hence 止 has been extended to mean "stop" and this has replaced the original meaning of "foot".

【部首】Radical　　止(stop)

【同部首字】Characters under the radical
　　正(right)，此(this)，步(step)

【词语】Words and phrases

止步	zhǐbù	halt; stop
止境	zhǐjìng	end; limit
止咳	zhǐké	relieve a cough
止渴	zhǐkě	quench one's thirst
止痛	zhǐtòng	relieve pain
止息	zhǐxī	cease; stop
止血	zhíxiě	stop bleeding

止步不前

zhǐ bù bù qián

stop the steps and no longer go ahead

i.e., stand still

止戈为武

zhǐ gē wéi wǔ

To stop the use of weapons and avoid war is truly military.

止水不波

zhǐ shuǐ bù bō

Still water does not have ripples.

i.e., a quiet mind

止谤莫若自修

zhǐ bàng mò ruò zì xiū

Nothing stop gossip as correcting one's own way.

【例句】 Example

我们的争论到此为止吧。

wǒ mén de zhēng lùn dào cǐ wéi zhǐ ba

Let's stop our argument here.

zhōng

(center; middle)

从"中"的字形（ 彣 ），便能猜到它有中间的意思。外部的"口"表示一定的范围，而（ 彐 ）便是放在"口"的正中间，表示不会超出其范围。

中 is also a pictograph character which shows a pole with some decorative streams (彐). In the middle there is a 口 indicating where the center is.

【部首】 Radical | (vertical line)

【同部首字】Characters under the radical
    甲(first)，丰(rich)

【词语】 Words and phrases

中餐	zhōngcān	Chinese food
中草药	zhōngcǎoyào	Chinese herbal medicine
中等	zhōngděng	middle; medium
中国	Zhōngguó	China
中立	zhōnglì	neutrality
中秋节	Zhōngqiūjié	the Chinese Mid-Autumn Festival
中文	Zhōngwén	Chinese language
中心	zhōngxīn	center; core
中学	zhōngxué	middle school

中流砥柱

zhōng liú dǐ zhù

firm rock in midstream

i.e., a tower of strength

中外古今

zhōng wài gǔ jīn

both ancient and modern, Chinese and foreign

中饱私囊

zhōng bǎo sī náng

line one's pocket with public funds or other people's money

中西合璧

zhōng xī hé bì

a good combination (blending) of Chinese and Western elements

中庸之道

zhōng yōng zhī dào

the doctrine of the mean

中看不中用

zhōng kàn bù zhōng yòng

be pleasant with eyes, but not agreeable to the palate

【例句】Example

园子的中间有一棵大树。

yuán zǐ de zhōng jiān yǒu yì kē dà shù

There is a big tree in the center of the garden.

众

zhòng

(many; numerous)

丿 | 人 | 𠆢 | 众 | 仒 | 众

从"众"（𨈿）的甲骨文中，你能看出在太阳（☉）的下面有三个人（𢓊）正在弯下腰工作吗？有趣的是，太阳后来变成了一只眼睛（👁）在看着很多人工作，所以"众"就是"很多"的意思。

Referring once again to ancient inscriptions found on the oracle bones, we find that 众 was comprised of two parts: the upper part is "the sun" (☉) and the lower part represents three people bending over working (𢓊), this being the original form and meaning of 众. As it developed through time the sun above the three people turned into an eye shape (👁), seeming to suggest a big eye watching over many people working. So "many" is the original meaning of 众.

【部首】Radical　　　人(person)

【同部首字】Characters under the radical
　　全(all)，令(order)，今(today)

【词语】Words and phrases

众多	zhòngduō	multitudinous
众人	zhòngrén	everybody
众生	zhòngshēng	all living creatures
众望	zhòngwàng	people's expectations

众所周知

    zhòng suǒ zhōu zhī

      as everybody knows

众目睽睽

    zhòng mù kuí kuí

      The eyes of the masses are fixed on somebody or something.

众矢之的

    zhòng shǐ zhī dì

      target of public criticism

众望所归

    zhòng wàng suǒ guī

      to enjoy popular confidence

众志成城

    zhòng zhì chéng chéng

      collective purpose forming a fortress

【例句】Example

    俗话说：众人拾柴火焰高。

      sú huà shuō:zhòng rén shí chái huǒ yàn gāo

        An old saying goes: When all people add fuel the flames rise high.

子

zǐ

(son)

⸍	了	子

这个字最初的时候，本来是描画一个头上有三络头发的小孩（  ），后来变成了一个手脚摇摆的婴儿（  ）。仔细看看这个古字的形象，像不像一个初生婴儿的样子？

In the oracle bones the character depicts a child with three hairs growing on its head ( ). Later it developed into another shape, like a new-born baby with legs swaddled in cloth bands and two arms waving ( ), evoking a lively image of a baby.

【部首】 Radical　　子(son)

【同部首字】 Characters under the radical
孔(hole)，存(exist)，孙(grandson)

【词语】 Words and phrases

弟子	dìzǐ	discipline
独生子	dúshēngzǐ	an only son
父子	fùzǐ	father and son
子女	zǐnǚ	son and daughter
子孙	zǐsūn	descendants
子夜	zǐyè	midnight

子肖其父

    zǐ xiāo qí fù

      The son is the very image of his father.

子子孙孙

    zǐ zǐ sūn sūn

      descendants

子孙后代

    zǐ sūn hòu dài

      generations to come

【例句】Example

    她的子女都在国外工作。

      tā de zǐ nǚ dōu zài guó wài gōng zuò

        Her sons and daughters are all working abroad.

自

zì

(self)

| ′ | ⺝ | ⺈ | 白 | 自 | 自 |

象形字里的"自"字，画了一个鼻子的正面（⺊），原来就是指"鼻子"。当我们用手指着自己的鼻子时，就有了"我"、"自己"的意思。

自 is a pictograph of a nose (⺊) which is seen from the front with nostrils and a bridge. So, originally it represented the nose. As Chinese people indicate "myself" by pointing to the nose, hence the meaning of this character became "self" or "oneself", and the original meaning for nose is no longer used.

【部首】Radical   自(self)

【同部首字】Characters under the radical

臭(bad smell)

【词语】 Words and phrases

自爱	zì'ài	self-respect
自白	zìbái	make clear of one's meaning or position
自卑	zìbēi	be self-abased
自称	zìchēng	to call oneself; profess to be (sth.)
自从	zìcóng	since
自大	zìdà	self-important
自动	zìdòng	voluntarily; automatic

自费	zìfèi	at one's own expense
自负	zìfù	think highly of oneself
自己	zìjǐ	oneself
自觉	zìjué	conscious

自顾不暇

zì gù bù xiá

be unable even to fend for oneself

i.e., much less look after others

自告奋勇

zì gào fèn yǒng

offer to undertake (a difficult or dangerous task)

i.e., volunteer to do sth. difficult

自给自足

zì jǐ zì zú

self sufficiency

自命不凡

zì mìng bù fán

consider oneself no ordinary being

自欺欺人

zì qī qī rén

deceive oneself as well as others

自强不息

zì qiáng bù xī

make unremitting efforts to improve oneself

自食其果

zì shí qí guǒ

eat one's own bitter fruit

i.e., reap what one has sown

自以为是

zì yǐ wéi shì

consider oneself (always) in the right

【例句】 Example

我是自费来读书的。

wǒ shì zì fèi lái dú shū de

I came to study at my own expense.

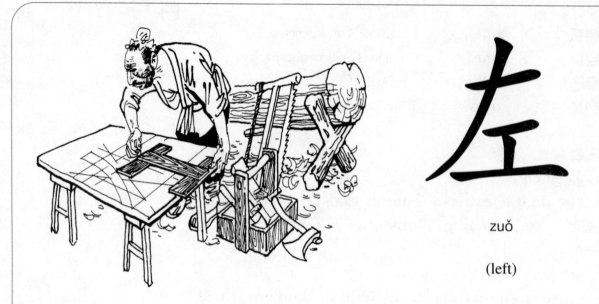

左

zuǒ

(left)

一　ナ　ナ　左　左

古时"左"字画的是一只左手（F）。后来这个字的右边加上了一把工匠用的尺（I），有协助、辅助的意思。

左 is a drawing of a left hand. In the oracle bones, the shape of this character was the same as the character "right hand" (F), except the fingers are reaching in the opposite direction. Later a drawing of a carpenter's ruler (I) was added under the hand, then it became a composite representation with a left hand holding a tool (F). This indicates "to help" or "to help working", which was the original meaning of the character.

【部首】Radical　　工(work)

【同部首字】Characters under the radical
　　巧(skilful)，差(bad)

【词语】Words and phrases

左边	zuǒbiān	the left
左面	zuǒmiàn	the left side
左派	zuǒpài	the left wing
左倾	zuǒqīng	left-leaning; inclined towards revolution
左手	zuǒshǒu	the left hand
左右	zuǒyòu	the left and right sides; around

左证 zuǒzhèng evidence

左顾右盼
　　zuǒ gù yòu pàn
　　　　glance right and left
左右逢源
　　zuǒ yòu féng yuán
　　　　be able to achieve success one way or another
左右为难
　　zuǒ yòu wéi nán
　　　　in a dilemma
左右开弓
　　zuǒ yòu kāi gōng
　　　　shoot first with one hand, then with the other
　　　　　　i.e., kick with both feet
左支右绌
　　zuǒ zhī yòu chù
　　　　not have enough money to cover the expenses
　　　　　　i.e., be unable to cope with a situation

【例句】Example
　　去机场的车站就在道路的左边。
　　　qù jī chǎng de chē zhàn jiù zài dào lù de zuǒ biān
　　　　The bus stop to the airport is to the left of the road.

图书推荐
Highlights

滚雪球学汉语
Snowballing Chinese

▶ 英法德西注释本
By joël Bel Lassen, Liu jialing
New words in English, French, German and Spanish
ISBN 9787802006430，128pp.
210×285 mm ￥48.00

MP3

新编基础汉语系列 （全三册）
New Approaches to Learning Chinese Series (3 volumes)
By Zhang Pengpeng

新编基础汉语　口语速成
Intensive Spoken Chinese (oral course)

▶ 汉英 Chinese-English edition (with MP3)
ISBN 9787800525773 ￥45.00

▶ 汉法 Chinese-French edition
ISBN 9787800528521 ￥29.80

▶ 汉西 Chinese-Spanish edition
ISBN 9787802003033 ￥29.80
185×250mm, 166pp 2CDs: ￥32.00

▶ 汉俄 Chinese-Russian edition
ISBN 9787802003002 ￥29.80

▶ 汉德 Chinese-German edition
ISBN 9787802003866 ￥29.80

▶ 汉阿 Chinese-Arabic edition
ISBN 9787802003835 ￥29.80

MP3

新编基础汉语 常用汉字部首
The Most Common Chinese Radicals (writing course)

▶ 汉英 Chinese-English edition
ISBN 9787800525766

▶ 汉法 Chinese-French edition
ISBN 7800528502

▶ 汉西 Chinese-Spanish edition
ISBN 9787802003040
185×258mm, 147pp ￥27.00

▶ 汉俄 Chinese-Russian edition
ISBN 9787802003019

▶ 汉德 Chinese-German edition
ISBN 9787802003873

▶ 汉阿 Chinese-Arabic edition
ISBN 9787802003842

新编基础汉语 集中识字
Rapid Literacy in Chinese (comprehensive course)

▶ 汉英 Chinese-English edition (with MP3)
ISBN 9787800526954 ￥39.00

▶ 汉法 Chinese-French edition (with MP3)
ISBN 9787800528514 ￥39.00

▶ 汉俄 Chinese-Russian edition
ISBN 9787802002999 ￥24.00
185×258mm, 136pp 2 CDs: ￥32.00

▶ 汉德 Chinese-German edition
ISBN 9787802003859 ￥24.00

▶ 汉阿 Chinese-Arabic edition
ISBN 9787802003828 ￥24.00

▶ 汉西 Chinese-Spanish edition
ISBN 9787802003026 ￥24.00

MP3

汉字五千年
Chinese Characters in Five Thousand Years

▶ 西文 Spanish edition
ISBN 9787802006454，Book ¥98.00
ISBN 9787887183040，DVD ¥168.00
▶ 德文 German edition
ISBN 9787802006461，Book ¥98.00
ISBN 9787887183033，DVD ¥168.00
170×225mm，250pp

MP3,CD-ROM

多媒体汉字卡片
Multimedia Cards of Chinese Characters

(8 packs of cards, 1 CD-ROM, 1 MP3)
145×210mm
▶ 汉英 Chinese-English edition
ISBN 7802000912 ¥298.00
▶ 汉西 Chinese-Spanish edition
ISBN 7802002214 ¥298.00
▶ 汉德 Chinese-German edition
ISBN 7802002222 ¥298.00
▶ 汉法 Chinese-French edition
ISBN 7802000041 ¥398.00

MP3,CD-ROM

看部首学汉字
Learn Chinese Characters by Radicals

▶ 汉英 Chinese-English edition
285×210mm，192pp
¥48.00

外国人汉字速成
500 Basic Chinese Characters—A Speedy Elementary Course

▶ 汉英 Chinese-English edition
ISBN 9787800524608，185×255mm，522pp
¥89.50

For more information, visit us at www.sinolingua.com.cn
Email: hyjx@sinolingua.com.cn **Tel:** 0086-10-68320585，68329621

选题策划：单　瑛
责任编辑：韩　晖
插图绘画：陶伟业
封面设计：胡　湖
印刷监制：佟汉冬

图书在版编目（CIP）数据

画说汉字.1 / 汪春，郑重庆编著. —北京：华语教学出版社，2005.7
ISBN 978-7-80200-101-5

Ⅰ. 画… Ⅱ. ①汪… ②郑… Ⅲ. 汉字—对外汉语教学—教学参考资料 Ⅳ. H195.4

中国版本图书馆 CIP 数据核字(2005)第065166号

画 说 汉 字

·（1）

汪 春　郑重庆　编著

*

©华语教学出版社有限责任公司
华语教学出版社有限责任公司出版
（中国北京百万庄大街24号　邮政编码100037）
电话：(86)10-68320585　68997826
传真：(86)10-68997826　68326333
网址：www.sinolingua.com.cn
电子信箱：hyjx@sinolingua.com.cn
新浪微博地址：http://weibo.com/sinolinguavip
北京密兴印刷有限公司印刷
2005 年（16开）第一版
2012 年第一版第四次印刷
（汉英）
ISBN 978-7-80200-101-5
9-CE-3676PA
定价：39.80 元